TIME OUT

RONAN SCULLY

Ballpoint Press

*To Jacqui, Mia and Sophie for always being
with me in prayer and thought*

Published in 2013 by Ballpoint Press
4 Wyndham Park, Bray, Co Wicklow, Republic of Ireland.
Telephone: 086 8217631
Email: ballpointpress1@gmail.com

ISBN 978-0-9572072-4-0

Book design and production by Elly Design

Printed and bound by GraphyCems

Front page photographs: Six people in Galway strike the 'time out' pose
Back page photograph: A tree in Ethiopia

~ CONTENTS ~

~ FOREWORD ~

Training for a marathon is a long and arduous business. It has some great moments but it also has many dark ones especially when the wind and rain are against you and you are a long way from home. It is almost always something small, something unusual, something intensely human that creates or inspires the energy and the desire to continue, to dig deep and to keep going until the end line becomes visible. Then the doubt, the fear, the physical and mental pain all fade away like magic and by crossing that line you have won the ultimate victory, you have beaten yourself.

One such memorable moment occurred during the second Dublin City marathon I participated in. Reaching the 21 mile stage I was passing over the flyover and suffering. Just as I got to the end of it a runner whom I had never seen before nor have seen since said as he passed me: "From now on we begin to enjoy ourselves". And I did.

Reading Ronan Scully's book is experiencing all his moments. They are personal to him. In his generosity of mind and spirit, he is sharing them with you. They are almost certainly not your moments but by reading them and experiencing them with him, you will undoubtedly remember similar moments that you have experienced. There is no greater gift than this.

Des Kenny
Kenny's Bookshop, Galway
www.kennys.ie

TIME OUT

~ INTRODUCTION ~

This designated Year of Faith is an apt time to see published this most readable book of reflections and photographs on the lived expression of communion with God and with one another. This year is a time to pause; a time for that reflective gaze that reveals to each one of us the God who dwells amongst us. TIME OUT is a fine title for this contemplative compilation and I salute both Ronan and Andrew on the depth of their thought. We need to dwell on the eternal in our midst and in these critical times to discover anew in our sisters and brothers the God who dwells amongst us.

There is a haunting line at the end of T.S. Eliot's, 'The Waste Land', "These fragments I have shored against my ruins." We are all aware of the ruins around us: the end of an era, the collapse of many traditions, the uncertainty about our roots, the loss of many anchors, the scepticism about any possible wisdom and the larger shadow of a world often in terrible pain. But my life has taught me to believe in humanity and God. The exploratory nature of these pages is meant to capture the unsteady roads of our seeking. Here are stabs at a vision, pointers at a surprise, avenues towards hope, faith and love – perhaps in that order. Faith itself is a God-given way of imagining existence – not a cold truth, easily captured in concepts. And my conviction is that these imaginative pieces, like prophecies, can deepen our angle of seeing.

These pages and pictures indicate the drama of life and they specialise in speaking to our intuitive levels of consciousness: They hit us below the belt of reason. They awaken wonder and develop it into wisdom. They confront pain by going further into depth.

Inevitably there are several important dimensions of faith that do not receive much attention in this book. Over 100 years ago the American thinker Josiah Royce wrote: 'My life means nothing, either theoretically or practically, unless I am a member of a community.'

This serves as a wise reminder that although the tone of these pages is personalist, our human roads towards light are never just private. The normal and blessed context for finding faith is within a community belonging. These thoughts will especially touch those on the inside of community in the hope of enriching their human basis for faith, but the hope is too that they will reach towards and help others reach towards those on the edges or outskirts of our community who walk more lonely paths of honest searching.

Self Help Africa and the Irish Guide Dogs for the Blind are to be the recipients of the funding raised by this venture and it is been kindly sponsored by David Lohan and published by Ballpoint Press. Thank you to all involved for so generously affording us the opportunity to ponder and wait on the disclosure of God's hidden love amongst us in the most ordinary and prosaic of moments. TIME OUT.

A Year of Faith. A blessed opportunity for each one of us.

Fr. Niall Ahern
Canon, Strandhill Parish, Co Sligo

ONE

MAKE EVERY DAY COUNT

Sometimes people come into our lives and we know right away that they were meant to be there, to serve some purpose, whether it is to teach us a lesson or to help us figure out who we are or who we want to become. Sometimes things happen to us that seem horrible, painful or unfair but on reflection we find that, without overcoming those obstacles, we would never have realised our potential, strength, willpower or true selves.

The people we meet who affect our lives, the success and downfalls we experience, help to create who we become. If someone loves you, give love back to them because they are teaching you to love and how to open your heart and eyes to things. If someone hurts you, betrays you, or breaks your heart, forgive them, for they have helped you learn about trust and the importance of being cautious. Make every day count. Appreciate every moment and take from those moments everything you possibly can for you may never be able to experience it again.

Talk to people that you have never talked to before, and listen to what they have to say. The following story might throw a little light on the subject. I heard it while at mass visiting a priest friend in St. Mary's parish in San Francisco during my time playing Gaelic football in the states.

❀ ❀ ❀

A group of alumni, highly established in their careers, got together to visit their old college professor. Conversation soon turned into complaints about stress in work and life.

Offering his guests tea, the professor went to the kitchen and returned with a large pot of tea and an assortment of cups-porcelain, plastic, glass, crystal – some plain looking, some expensive, some exquisite. He told his guests to help themselves to the tea.

After everyone had a cup of tea in hand, the professor said: "If you noticed, all the nice looking, expensive cups have been taken up, leaving behind the plain and cheap ones.

"While it is normal for you to want only the best for yourselves, that is also the source of your problems and stress. Be assured that the cup adds no quality to the tea. In most cases, it is just more expensive and in some cases, even hides what we drink.

"What all of you really wanted was tea. But you consciously went for the best cups. And then you began eyeing each other's cups, to see who had the best one.

"Now consider this. Life is the tea. The jobs, money, and position in society are the cups. They are just tools to hold and contain life. And the type of cup we have does not define, or change the quality of life we live.

"Sometimes by concentrating only on the cup, we fail to enjoy the tea. You should savour the tea, not the cups. The happiest people that I know in my circle of life don't have the best of everything. They just make the best of everything."

> **A MOMENT IN TIME**
> *Look at ways you can bring peace and joy into the lives of people who need it and try as much as you can to live a life of deep love and care.*

TWO

TRUE FRIENDS

I was thinking recently about friendship and what it means. Most people walk in and out of your life. But only true friends leave footprints in your heart.

When we look back on our younger years, we remember those who went to school with us, the people who made us laugh, the people who hung out with us when nobody else would and those who made our lives much better simply by being a part of it.

Good friends are hard to find, harder to leave, and impossible to forget. The language of friendship is not in words but in its meanings.

There is a beautiful story about friendship given to me involving a young boy and a puppy.

A shopkeeper hung a sign above his door that read 'Puppies for Sale'. A little boy appeared at the sign. 'How much are you going to sell those puppies for?' he asked. The owner replied: 'Anywhere from €20 to €30.' The little boy reached into his pocket and pulled out some change. 'I have €2.50. Can I have a look at them?'

The shopkeeper smiled and whistled. Out of the kennel came Pepsi, who ran down the aisle of the store followed by five teeny, tiny balls of fur. One puppy was lagging considerably behind. Immediately the little boy singled out the lagging, limping puppy and said: What's wrong with that little dog?'

The man explained that when the puppy was born, he had no hip socket and would limp for the rest of his life. The little boy got really excited and repeated: 'That's the puppy I want to buy!' The man replied, 'No, you don't want to buy that little dog. If you really want him, I'll give him to you.'

The little boy got quite upset. He looked straight into the man's eyes, and said: 'I don't want you to give him to me. He is worth every bit as much as the other dogs and I'll pay the full price. In fact, I'll give you €2.37 now and 50 cent every month until I have him paid for.'

The man countered: 'You really don't want to buy this puppy. He is never going to be able to run, jump and play like other puppies.' To this the little boy reached down and rolled up the leg of his trousers to reveal a badly-twisted, crippled left leg supported by a big metal brace. He looked up at the man and said: 'Well, I don't run so well myself and the little puppy will need someone who understands.'

A MOMENT IN TIME
Be thankful and cherish those true friends that are part of your life and understand that we all need help now and then.

THREE

LOVE FROM YOUR HEART

Loving and living deeply from the heart is not easy. It takes hard work. It demands self-sacrifice, a generous spirit, and an expansive embrace. It implies the risk of loving and living without barriers and obstacles. It suggests walking in someone else's shoes, leaving behind one's own baggage that makes the walk heavier and letting go of old habits that become burdens on the journey. Loving and living deeply from the heart is intentional. It doesn't happen accidentally. It happens because we decide to live that way. It loves in spite of us even if it hurts. It means getting beyond what holds us back. Loving and living deeply from the heart is about forgiveness. It forgives previous generations for their actions.

Deep-hearted love does not just contemplate the wrongs that have been done or the mistakes that have been made. It also calls us to active repentance. It says: "Don't just sit there feeling bad; do something to make it better." It gets beyond that which keeps us stuck in the past and prevents us from moving into the future.

Your biggest weakness can become your biggest strength.

Take, for example, the story of one 10-year-old boy who decided to study judo despite the fact that he had lost his left arm in a devastating car accident. The boy began lessons with an old Japanese judo master. The boy was doing well, so he couldn't understand why, after three months of training, the master had taught him only one move. "Sensei," the boy finally said, "shouldn't I be learning more moves?"

"This is the only move you know, but this is the only move you'll ever need to know," the Sensei replied. Several months later he went to his first tournament. Surprising himself, the boy easily won his first two matches. The third match proved to be more difficult, but after some time, his opponent became impatient and charged; the boy deftly used his one move to win the match. The boy was now in the finals.

This time, his opponent was bigger and more experienced. The boy appeared to be overmatched. Concerned that the boy might get hurt, the referee called a time-out. He was about to stop the match when the Sensei intervened. "No," the Sensei insisted, "let him continue." Soon after the match resumed, his opponent made a critical mistake – he dropped his guard. Instantly, the boy used his move to pin him.

The boy had won the match and the tournament. He was the champion.

On the way home, the boy and Sensei reviewed every move in each and every match. Then the boy summoned the courage to ask what was really on his mind. 'Sensei, how did I win the tournament with only one move?"

"You won for two reasons," the Sensei answered. "First, you've almost mastered one of the most difficult throws in all of judo. Second, the only known defence for that move is for your opponent to grab your left arm."

The boy's biggest weakness had become his biggest strength.

A MOMENT IN TIME
Don't just watch quietly, do something. But whatever you do, do it with love, for it is only in loving and living deeply from the heart, that we and our precious earth and all who dwell therein, will have a chance for the future.

FOUR

MAKE THE MOST OF WHAT YOU'VE GOT

I read something funny yet true recently about life: "It is a funny thing but if you refuse to accept anything but the best, you very often get it".

It is very apt in today's world also. Often we do not care about ourselves and do not live each moment to the best of our abilities. We settle for second best. If our inner heart has holes, we do not bother to refill them, thinking how does it matter? The truth is your body can feel it and you know it matters. Many times, we skip meals thinking it doesn't matter and you think I have more important things to do in life. Truth is, your body needs that nourishment. No one else is going to nourish your body but you. For the world to treat you well, you need to treat yourself well. If you have no pride in yourself, chances are the world will look at you in the same way.

It is said that charity begins at home. We care for the less fortunate and the needy which is a great quality in any human being. But remember your mind, body and soul need you first. Pamper yourself, enjoy life to the full and make the most of what you have got. It is said that if you keep a clean home, nourish your body, pamper yourself, you will feel blessed. But most of us do not invest time in ourselves. We are so absorbed by the outside world that we forget.

Most of us feel it is a sheer waste of time to do it anyway. Pampering yourself is vanity, we think. Well, overdoing it might be vanity but doing something you like once in a while is important to feel good in life. Everything affects everything. The way you walk affects the way you talk. The way you dress affects the way you feel. The care you give to yourself will affect how you care about others. Nurturing and feeling good about yourself is the first step towards confidence and goes a long way in fulfilling your ambitions. There are positive vibrations all around you. You just need to grab them and realise them. For this, you need to have strength and confidence in yourself. Be happy to make others happy. This story might help to explain what I mean.

❧ ❧ ❧

'The park bench was deserted as I sat down to read, beneath the long, straggly branches of an old willow tree. Disillusioned by life with good reason to frown, for the world was intent on dragging me down. And if that weren't enough to ruin my day, a young boy approached me, all tired from play. He stood right before me with his head tilted down and said with great excitement: "Look what I found."

In his hand was a flower, and what a pitiful sight, with its petals all worn – not enough rain, or too little light. Wanting him to take his dead flower and go off to play, I faked a small smile and then shifted away. But instead of retreating he sat next to my side and declared with overacted surprise: "It smells lovely and it's beautiful, too. That's why I picked it; here, it's for you."

The weed before me was dying or dead, not vibrant of colours: orange, yellow or red. But I knew I must take it or he might never leave. So I reached for the flower, and replied: "Thanks, just what I need."

But instead of placing the flower in my hand, he held it mid-air. It was then that I noticed for the very first time that the boy was blind. I heard my voice quiver, tears shone in the sun as I thanked him for picking the very best one. "You're welcome," he smiled, and then ran off to play; unaware of the impact he'd had on my day. I sat there and wondered how he managed to see a self-pitying man beneath an old willow tree.

How did he know of my self-indulged plight? Perhaps from his heart, he'd been blessed with true sight.

Through the eyes of a blind child, at last I could see the problem was not with the world; the problem was me. And for all of those times I myself had been blind, I vowed to see the beauty in life, and appreciate every second that's mine. And then I held that wilted flower up to my nose and breathed in the fragrance of a beautiful rose. And smiled, as I watched that young boy, another weed in his hand, about to change the life of another unsuspecting old man.

A MOMENT IN TIME
Celebrate who you are. We are here to inspire one another, to help one another, to share with one another. Treasure your life and the lives of those around you. We are all in this together.

TIME OUT

FIVE

ALWAYS BE YOURSELF

Embrace that person inside you that has ideas and strengths like no one else. Be the person you know yourself to be. And above all, be true to yourself and put your heart in it.

Starting this week get your priorities right. Years from now it won't really matter what you did today. What will matter is how you loved and cared and how you applied this to life. Take full responsibility for your ambitions. Know your worth. Don't expect to see positive changes if you surround yourself with negative and destructive people. Don't give part-time people a full-time position in your life. Know your value and what you have to offer and never settle for anything less than what you deserve. Treat people the way you would like to be treated

When faced with long queues, traffic jams or waiting on an appointment, you have two choices: You can get frustrated, or you can view it as life's way of giving you a guilt-free break from rushing, and spend that time daydreaming, conversing or watching nature. The first choice will raise your blood pressure. The second choice will raise your perception. Choose the things that truly matter. The smartest way to live is choosing what truly matters, and pursuing it passionately.

Let someone love you just the way you are. As flawed as you might be, as unattractive as you sometimes feel, and as unaccomplished as you think you are, let someone love you despite all of this; and let that someone be you. Accept your strengths and weaknesses. We often waste too much time comparing ourselves to others and wishing to be something else. Everybody has their own strengths and weaknesses, and it is only when we accept everything, then we are able to become who we are capable of being. Learn from others, and move on when you must.

Some people come into your life as blessings; others come into your life as lessons. Be honest in your relationships. If you're not happy, be honest, and move on if you must. When you're truly in love, being faithful isn't a sacrifice, it's a joy. Don't get to the end of your life and find that you lived one of regrets. When it comes to living as a passionate, inspired human being, the only challenge greater than learning to walk a mile in someone else's shoes, is learning to walk a lifetime comfortably in your own.

A MOMENT IN TIME

Never give up on you. This is your life; shape it. Strength shows not only in the ability to hold on but in the ability to start over. It is never too late to become what you might have been.

SIX

A MOTHER'S LOVE IS A BLESSING

A few months ago I attended the funeral of the mother of a friend of mine. I witnessed his great loss but also the great love he had for his mother. It made me realise the love I had for my mother but more importantly the love my mother has for me.

Mothers hold a sacred place in all our hearts. I imagine that the longer you enjoy your mother's love and friendship, the harder it is when the time comes to say goodbye. Real heroes live in our midst and in a lot of cases it is mothers, who by silently giving and encouraging, enable others to grow and to blossom. I saw a real life story of a mother's love in Ethiopia recently; it might help to shine a little light on why a mother's love is a blessing.

Yeabsira had been battling for her life at an emergency nutrition camp in drought-affected Ethiopia operated by Irish missionaries. I was so grateful for the staff of her camp that made this programme possible. She wouldn't have had a chance otherwise. As I sat by her mother Etsub, my only thought was to comfort her and her daughter as she told me of their hardship and suffering due to the drought in that part of Ethiopia. The small puppet I played with put a faint smile on Yeabsira's sunken face. Like far too many families in Yeabsira's village, her family lost much of their herd when the rains failed for two years. It meant the animals produced a fraction of the milk they once supplied.

"We were doing everything we could to support our family," Etsub explained. "We were just scraping by when Yeabsira got sick." Malnutrition weakened the little girl and a cold escalated to pneumonia. Yeabsira became a shadow of her former self, weighing 12 pounds – about half of her ideal healthy weight. Etsub faithfully fought for her daughter's life – feeding her fortified milk and porridge day and night.

Constantly by her side, staying with her and sleeping on a small gurney in the camp. Etsub knows the pain of losing a daughter; Yeabsira's three-year-old sister died from hunger. Her sorrow washed over me as I saw her lips quiver and tears streams down her cheeks. She wept silently, not wanting to upset Yeabsira. "I will not lose her," she said fiercely. I told Etsub the camps health workers brought me to see Yeabsira's progress. In just a few short days, she gained more than two pounds and was on the road to recovery. "I've no words to describe how grateful I am to the Irish missionaries in the emergency camp," she said, pressing her hand to her heart.

❀ ❀ ❀

Mothers certainly feel all our pain. It's like when a little boy asked his mother, "Why are you crying?"

"Because I'm a woman," she told him. "I don't understand," he said.

His mum just hugged him and said, "And you never will." Later the little boy asked his father, "Why does mammy cry for no reason?"

"All women cry for no reason," was all his dad said.

The little boy grew up and became a man, still wondering why women cry. Finally he prayed to God who would surely know the answer. When God responded he asked, "God, why do women cry so easily?" God said: "When I made the woman she had to be made special. I made her shoulders strong enough to carry the weight of the world, yet gentle enough to give comfort. I gave her an inner strength to endure childbirth and the rejection that many times comes from her children. I gave her a hardness that allows her to keep going when everyone else gives up, and take care of her family through sickness and fatigue without complaining. I gave her the sensitivity to love her children under any and all circumstances, even when her child has hurt her very badly. I gave her strength to carry her husband through his faults and fashioned her from his rib to protect his heart. I gave her wisdom to know that a good husband never hurts his wife, but sometimes tests her strengths and her resolve to stand beside him unfalteringly. And lastly, I gave her a tear to shed. This is hers and only hers exclusively to use whenever she needs it. She needs no reason, no explanation, it's hers."

"You see my son," said God, "the beauty of a woman is not in the clothes she wears, the figure that she carries, or the way she combs her hair. The beauty of a woman must be seen in her eyes, because that is the doorway to her heart – the place where love resides."

A MOMENT IN TIME

Make your mother and the mother of your children feel the most special woman in the world by showing your care, love and affection. Most of all let your mother know how much you love her for life is short and time is running out.

TIME OUT

SEVEN

A JAPANESE MOTHER'S SACRIFICE

My friends Paul and his wife Mary were so moved by the earthquake and devastation that hit the country of Japan that they organised a 'Japan Fundraiser weekend' in their Kings Head venue in Galway to raise much needed funds to help the people affected by this unimaginable disaster.

They were well supported by RTE 2FM's Hector Ó hEochagáin who helped rally the troops so that the message of what happened in Japan could be heard and that people could show their solidarity to by raising much needed funds and awareness of their plight.

The news on that day in March was full of bulletins and talk, but the 8.9-magnitude earthquake and subsequent tsunami that hit Japan early that Friday morning almost defied speech. It is a nice illusion that our world is stable. We choose to believe it and hope for it most of the time. We accept and are comforted by the changes of the seasons and the rising and setting of the sun. These things seem predictable. They're not.

As the recent disasters in Haiti, New Zealand, The Horn of Africa and Japan remind us, we are fragile beings in a world ruled by the still-unpredictable forces of nature. For those of us who watched on our TVs, what happened in Japan is almost unimaginable. For those who were caught in it, it was all too real.

Another thing that is 'real' and that nothing can come close to is the love that a mother feels for her children. Most women are inherently excellent mothers. Women carry their young before they are born and then continue to nurture them throughout their childhood and even into adulthood. Mothers make sure that their children are safe and happy throughout their childhood. It is the unconditional love that a mother feels which drives these feelings. It is hard to describe the feeling that a mother has towards her children.

Raising children comes with its own share of frustrations. From the needy new-born baby that requires regular care to the sullen teenager, a mother's job is anything but easy.

There is a saying that: "God could not be everywhere and so he invented mothers." A mother puts her children before anything else, including her own comfort and happiness. As the following true story from a Japanese newspaper written shortly after the earthquake will testify even when things are not going well a mother will always put the safety of her child before everything else.

After the Earthquake had subsided, when the rescuers reached the ruins of a young woman's house, they saw her dead body through the cracks. But her pose was somehow strange that she knelt on her knees like a person who was worshiping; her body was leaning forward, and her two hands were supported by an object. The collapsed house had crashed on her back and her head. With so many difficulties, the leader of the rescuer team put his hand through a narrow gap on the wall to reach the woman's body. He was hoping that this woman could be still alive. However, the cold and stiff body told him that she had passed away for sure. He and the rest of the team left this house and were going to search the next collapsed building. For some reason, the team leader went back, knelt down and used his hand through the narrow cracks to search the little space under the dead body. Suddenly, he screamed with excitement. A child.

There is a child alive in there.

The whole team worked together; carefully they removed the piles of ruined objects around the dead woman. There was a three-month-old little boy wrapped in a flowery blanket under his mother's dead body. Obviously, the woman had made the ultimate sacrifice for saving her son. When her house was falling, she used her body to make a cover to protect her son. The little boy was still sleeping peacefully when the team leader picked him up. The medical doctor came quickly to examine the little boy. After he opened the blanket, he saw a cell phone inside the blanket. There was a text message on the screen. It read: "If you can survive, you must remember that I love you."

This cell phone was passing around from one hand to another. Every body that read the message wept. "If you can survive, you must remember that I love you." Such is the mother's love for her child!

A MOMENT IN TIME

Remember what the famous writer Pascal wrote: "The least movement is of importance to all nature. The entire ocean is affected by a pebble." Pray for those suffering still in Japan, Haiti, The Horn of Africa.

TIME OUT

EIGHT

HONESTY IN EVERYDAY LIFE

Honesty is being frank, forthright and accurate in presenting reality as you see it. It is being straight forward in revealing what you know or believe. It is being candid in giving out information that is accurate and complete. Honesty is feeling that you have nothing to hide and that you can say what's in your heart. It's being comfortable in revealing what you know by being upfront and "telling it like it is".

It's being able to say how much you know and how much you don't know, and includes always being able to say "I don't know", when that is the case. Honesty has both a doing side and a knowing side. The doing side is being forthright in saying what you believe. The knowing side is recognising honesty, both in you and in others. It knows when someone is being honest with you. It also knows when you are being honest with yourself, so that you don't delude yourself by refusing to see your own truth. A story I heard at a retreat might shine a little light on what I am trying to say.

A successful businessman was growing old and knew it was time to choose a successor to take over the business. Instead of choosing one of his directors, he decided to do something different. He called all the young executives together. He said: "It's time for me to step down and choose the next CEO. I have decided to choose one of you."

The young executives were shocked, but the boss continued. "I am going to give each one of you a SEED today – one very special SEED. I want you to plant the seed, water it and come back here one year from today with what you have grown from the seed I have given you. I will then judge the plants that you bring, and the one I choose will be the next CEO."

One guy, named Gary, was there that day and he, like the others, received a seed. He went home and excitedly told his wife. She helped him get a pot and soil and he planted the seed. Everyday he would water it and watch to see if it had grown. After about three weeks, some of the other executives began to talk about their seeds and the plants that were beginning to grow. Gary kept checking his seed but nothing ever grew. Three more weeks went by, still nothing. Gary felt like a failure. Six months went by – still nothing. Gary didn't say anything to his colleagues, he just kept watering and fertilising the soil – he so wanted the seed to grow.

A year finally went by and all the young executives of the company brought their plants to the CEO for inspection. Gary told his wife that he wasn't going to take an empty pot. She told him to be honest about what happened. Gary felt sick to his stomach, but he knew his wife was right. He took his empty pot to the boardroom. When he arrived, he was amazed at the beauty and variety of plants grown by the other executives. Gary put his empty pot on the floor and many of his colleagues laughed. When the CEO arrived, he greeted everyone. "My, what great plants and flowers you have grown," said the CEO.

All of a sudden, the CEO spotted Gary at the back of the room with his empty pot. He ordered Gary to the front. When Gary got there, he told his story. The CEO asked everyone to sit down except Gary. He looked at Gary and then announced to the young executives.

"Behold your next Chief Executive Officer. His name is

Gary." Gary couldn't believe it. "How could he be the new CEO?" the others asked in bewilderment.

Then the CEO explained: "One year ago today, I gave everyone in this room a seed. I told you to take the seed, plant it, water it, and bring it back to me today. But I gave you all boiled seeds; they were dead – it was not possible for them to grow. All of you, except Gary, have brought me plants and flowers. When you found that the seed would not grow, you substituted another seed for the one I gave you. Gary was the only one with the courage and honesty to bring me a pot with my seed in it. Therefore, he is the one who will be the new Chief Executive Officer."

A MOMENT IN TIME

If you plant honesty, you will reap trust, if you plant goodness, you will reap friends. If you plant humility, you will reap greatness. If you plant perseverance, you will reap contentment. If you plant consideration, you will reap perspective. If you plant hard work, you will reap success. If you plant forgiveness, you will reap reconciliation. So, be careful what you plant now; it will determine who you will be in the future.

TIME OUT

NINE

MAKE TIME TO CARE

We each have the power to affect the world we live in. There are so many ways to apply love and care in our everyday lives. Yet, if we do not love and take care of ourselves, it is virtually impossible to feel and share love and genuine care with the world around us.

If we can practise constant acts of love and care, then we can bring genuine love and care upon ourselves and our world. Forgiveness is the easiest and most powerful act of love and care you can make. Both for you and for others, this activity promotes unity, harmony and oneness that transform the old into the new. I have experienced that recently when I was forgiven unconditionally by some family members for letting them down and for being so out of line in my dealings with them.

Our beautiful world is filled with opportunities to experience love, tolerance, peace and joy. When we, as individuals, realise our potential to love and care unconditionally, we transform ourselves and our world at the same time. Such is the power we wield every moment of every day. The choice is ours to create a world of love, genuine care and goodwill. Every moment of every day is a new beginning. Each moment holds a new beginning of possibility and an opportunity to create without limitation. We can let go of what we perceive or believe is before us and allow our personal potential to shine through.

Try to start each day as a new journey of self-discovery. Let go of yesterday and tomorrow and embrace the power of the present moment and try to remind yourself daily of the newness of life, which in itself is a form of prayer and of thanksgiving.

❁ ❁ ❁

I read a book lately by Bob Moorehead that talked to me about the paradoxes that now face us in our daily living. It points out that we have taller buildings but shorter tempers, wider roads, but narrower viewpoints. We spend more, but have less, we buy more, but enjoy less. We have bigger houses and smaller families, more conveniences but less time. We have more degrees but less sense, more knowledge, but less judgment, more experts, yet more problems, more medicine but less wellness. We drink too much, smoke too much, laugh too little, drive too fast, get too angry, stay up too late, get up too tired, read too little, watch TV too much, and pray too seldom.

We have multiplied our possessions but reduced our values. We talk too much, love too seldom, and hate too often. We've learned how to make a living but not a life. We've added years to life, not life to years. We've been all the way to the moon and back but have trouble crossing the street to meet a new neighbour. We conquered outer space but not inner space. We've done larger things but not better things. We've cleaned up the air, but polluted the soul. We've conquered the atom but not our prejudice. We write more but learn less. We plan more but accomplish less. We've learned to rush but not to wait.

We build more computers to hold more information, to produce more copies than ever but we communicate less and less. These are the times of fast foods and slow digestion, big men and small character, steep profits and shallow relationships. These are the days of two incomes but more divorce, fancier houses, but broken homes. These are days of quick trips, disposable diapers, throwaway morality, one night stands, overweight bodies and pills that do everything from cheer, to quiet, to kill.

It is a time when there is much in the showroom window and nothing in the stockroom. A time when technology can bring this A Moment In Time to you, and a time when you can choose either to share this insight or to just throw it away.

A MOMENT IN TIME
Say 'I love you' to your partner and your loved ones but most of all mean it. A kiss and an embrace will mend hurt when it comes from deep inside of you.

TIME OUT

TEN

PLAYING FIELDS OF LIFE

I've often been to Croke Park to watch the various Gaelic football and hurling matches, mostly with my dad. It's been an integral part of our father-son relationship for as long as I can remember. I enjoy it and love to watch how each manager interacts with their team and how each player interacts with their manager. The better the interaction, the better chance they seem to have of winning on the playing field. It always reminds me of a story a Galway footballer told me.

A stranger was walking by the Pearse Stadium GAA pitch in Salthill. He stopped to watch four kids trying to kick the football over the bar. The football bounced to where the stranger was standing. He grabbed the football and kicked it high. The stranger was standing at least 65 yards away from the goal. The football went straight over the black spot of the goal. The kids went wild roaring, 'no way!' and 'lucky shot'.

The stranger yelled out: 'One more shot,' to which one kid replied, 'Ain't no way he can do two. The wind is blowing.' One of the kids kicked the football down to where the stranger was standing. He kicked the football high again. The football again went straight over the black spot. The kids were stunned. One kid kicked the football toward the stranger again. The stranger lofted the football up in the air the same way with the same result. 'You boys want to learn how to be top footballers?'

One kid asked, 'Who are you, man?' The stranger, drawing nearer, said: 'I'm just passing through. Want to learn how to play football? I'll show you how.' The stranger worked with each kid showing him how to improve his football. Every kid improved immediately. It got so the kids couldn't miss.

Suddenly, the stranger disappeared. Three of the four boys looked around and saw only an empty green field. One of the kids mouth had dropped wide open. He was frozen in place. They were sure they had seen a ghost. Suddenly the stranger reappeared out of thin air. 'I am not a ghost. I do what the manager tells me to do. Today I am a teacher, teaching you how to play football and other things about life. I taught you how to play football but I also taught you about more important things than football. Remember I taught you if you don't have a goal, you don't have a game. I taught you unless you pass the football and share the scoring you lose. I taught you if you do not follow the rules, you can't win. I taught you that you have to be honest with yourself. You need to know what you can and can't do. I taught you to develop the part of your game you do best. I taught you to defend against the bad things of life and attack to keep the good things going.

'I taught you to improve your game and improve your character. I taught you not to repeat mistakes in your game but to eliminate the mistakes as soon as you can. You must quickly eliminate the mistakes, so the mistakes do not become a habit. I taught you to put others before yourself.

'One more thing, you must always talk to the manager. If you don't talk to the manager, the manager won't talk to you,' he said before disappearing again.

The boys froze. One young lad said, 'I think my mother sent this guy.' Another added: 'No, your mother wouldn't send a strange guy to teach us to play football. She'd send Ray Silke, or Alan Mullholland, or Padraig Joyce, or some other famous football star.' They all kind of laughed but the child persisted and said: 'No, my mother is always praying for me. My mother is always talking to the manager about life.'

A MOMENT IN TIME

See where you need help from your manager. Listen to what he or she is telling you and try your best to get a good result. Believe in yourself to always play well on the playing fields of life.

TIME OUT

ELEVEN

BELIEVE AND BE THE DIFFERENCE

What a few emotional days we had in the Scully household when our eldest daughter Mia started school. It's a huge occasion, especially, I suppose, when it's the first child in the family. It's one of those special milestones in life. It was a great first week for Mia, thank God, and we hope and pray it will continue for all children and young people going to school and third level. I hope that they, their teachers and lecturers, enjoy everything that they do and learn. An inspirational anonymous story might help to explain my thoughts on how sometimes children can teach us a lot.

As Mrs O'Connell stood in front of her 5th class on the very first day of school, she told the children a lie. Like most teachers, she looked at her students and said that she loved them all the same. But that was impossible, because there in the front row, slumped in his seat, was a little boy named Niall Mac.

Mrs O'Connell had watched Niall the year before and noticed that he didn't play well with the other children, that his clothes were messy and that he constantly needed a bath. It got to the point where Mrs O'Connell would actually take delight in marking his papers with a broad red pen putting a big 'F' at the top of his papers.

At the school where Mrs O'Connell taught, she was required to review each child's past records and she put Niall off until last. However, when she reviewed his file, she was in for a surprise. Niall's first class teacher wrote: "Niall is a bright child with a hearty laugh. He does his work neatly and has good manners...he is a joy to be around."

His second class teacher wrote: "Niall is an excellent student, well liked by his classmates but he is troubled because his mother has a terminal illness and life at home must be a struggle."

His third class teacher wrote: "His mother's death had been hard on him. He tries to do his best but his father doesn't show much interest and his home life will soon affect him if some steps aren't taken."

Niall's fourth class teacher wrote: "Niall is withdrawn and doesn't show much interest in school. He doesn't have many friends and he sometimes sleeps in class."

By now, Mrs O'Connell realised the problem and she was ashamed of herself.

She felt even worse when her students brought her Christmas presents, wrapped in beautiful paper, except for Niall's. His present was clumsily wrapped in a brown paper bag. Mrs O'Connell took pains to open it in the middle of the other presents. Some of the children started to laugh when she found a rhinestone bracelet with some of the stones missing and a bottle that was half full of perfume.

But she stifled the children's laughter when she exclaimed how pretty the bracelet was and dabbing some of the perfume on her wrist. Niall Mac stayed after school that day just long enough to say: "Mrs O'Connell, you looked just like my mum today and you smelled just like she used to."

After the children left, she cried. On that very day, she quit teaching reading, and writing, and arithmetic. Instead, she began to teach children. Mrs O'Connell paid particular attention to Niall. As she worked with him, his mind seemed to come alive. By the end of the year, Niall had become one of the smartest children in the class and, despite her lie that she would love all the children the same, Niall became one of her "teacher's pets."

A year later, she found a note under her door, from Niall, telling her that she was still the best teacher he ever had. Six years went by before she got another note from Niall. He then wrote that he had finished secondary school, third in his class and she was still the best teacher he ever had. Four years after that, she got another letter, saying that while things had been tough at times, he'd stayed in school and would soon graduate from NUIG with the highest of honours. He assured Mrs O'Connell that she was still the best and favourite teacher he ever had.

Then four more years passed and yet another letter came. This time he explained that after he got his bachelor's degree, he decided to go a little further. But now his name was a little longer – the letter was signed, Niall F. Mac MD.

The story doesn't end there. You see, there was yet another letter that spring. Niall said he'd met this girl and was going to be married. He explained that his father had died a couple of years previously and he was wondering if Mrs O'Connell might agree to sit in the place at the wedding that was usually reserved for the mother of the groom. Of course, Mrs O'Connell did. And guess what? She wore that bracelet, the one with several rhinestones missing. And she made sure she was wearing the perfume that Niall remembered his mother wearing on their last Christmas together.

They hugged each other, and Dr Mac whispered in Mrs O'Connell's ear: "Thank you Mrs O'Connell for believing in me. Thank you so much for making me feel important and showing me that I could make a difference."

Mrs O'Connell, with tears in her eyes, whispered back. She said, "Niall, you have it all wrong. You were the one who taught me that I could make a difference. I didn't know how to teach until I met you."

A MOMENT IN TIME

Let us all try as much as possible to make a difference for the good in one another's life's as much as we can, for we all need help and support and indeed our country needs us all to make a difference for the good of one another as we continue to face into the dreadful economic situation that we find ourselves in.

TWELVE

THE IMPORTANCE OF FORGIVENESS

When was the last time you felt let down by someone? Did you feel like taking revenge on that person and wanted to show that justice really does exist. You are a true saint if at some time you've not thought about responding angrily to someone that has harmed you in someway. This is hate and it slowly kills you from the inside.

Nearly all of us at sometime have been hurt by the actions or words of another. These wounds can leave you with bitter feelings but if you don't practise forgiveness, you may be the one who pays most dearly. By embracing forgiveness, you embrace peace, hope, and joy.

Forgiveness is a decision to let go of anger and resentment. The act that hurt you may always remain a part of your life but forgiveness can lessen its grip on you and help you focus on positive parts of your life. Forgiveness doesn't mean that you deny the other persons responsibility for hurting you and it doesn't minimise or justify the wrong. You can forgive the person without excusing the act. Forgiveness brings a kind of peace that helps you go on with life. Letting go of hurts makes way for compassion, kindness and peace and can lead to healthier relationships with less stress in your life. Forgiveness is a commitment to a process of change.

A way to begin is by recognising the value of forgiveness and its importance in your life at a given time. Then reflect on the facts of the situation, how you've reacted, and how this combination has affected your life, health and well-being. When you're ready, actively choose to forgive the person who has offended you. Move away from your role of victim and release the control and power the offending person and situation have had in your life.

As you let go of hurts, you'll no longer define your life by how you've been hurt. You may even find compassion and understanding.

❀ ❀ ❀

A story I heard when in India might help to explain what I am trying to relay. 'Once upon a time two brothers, who lived on adjoining farms, fell into conflict with one another. It was the first serious rift in 40 years of farming side by side, sharing machinery, and trading labour and goods. Then the long collaboration fell apart. It began with a small misunderstanding and it grew into a major difference, and finally it exploded into an exchange of bitter words followed by weeks of silence.

One morning there was a knock on the older brother's door. He opened it to find a man with a carpenter's toolbox. 'I'm looking for a few days work,' the man said. 'Perhaps you would have a few small jobs here and there. Could I help you?'

'Yes,' said the older brother. 'I do have a job for you. Look across the creek to that farm. That's my neighbour, in fact it's my younger brother. Last week there was a meadow between us and he took his bulldozer to the river levee and now there is a lake between us. Well, he may have done this to spite me, but I'll go one better. See that pile of lumber curing by the barn? I want you to build a fence, an eight foot fence so I won't need to see his place anymore. That will show him. The carpenter said: 'I think I understand the situation. Show me the nails and the digger and I'll be able to do a job that pleases you.'

The older brother had to go to town for supplies to help the carpenter get the materials ready and then he went off for the day. The carpenter worked hard for hours measuring, sawing and nailing. About sunset when the farmer returned, the carpenter had just finished the job. The farmer's jaw dropped. There was no fence there at all. Instead there was a bridge stretching from one side of the lake to the other. A fine piece of work, handrails and all, and the neighbour, his younger brother was at that moment coming across the bridge with his arms outstretched.

'You are quite a fellow to build this bridge after all I've said about you.' The two brothers met at the middle of the bridge, hugging each other. They turned to see the carpenter hoist his toolbox on his shoulder. 'No, wait. Stay a few days. I've lots of other projects for you,' said the older brother.

'I'd love to stay on,' the carpenter said, 'but I have so many more bridges to build.'

Forgiveness is a crucial part of any meaningful relationship. We are all human and fallible. Despite our best efforts, we will do things that hurt someone else. We all need forgiveness from time to time. When someone you love hurts you deeply, the natural instinct is to lash out. However, achieving true forgiveness ultimately helps you and your relationship much more. It takes a stronger person to forgive than to attack.

I heard this prayer recently about forgiveness. 'Let the rain come and wash away the ancient grudges, the bitter hatreds held and nurtured over generations. Let the rain wash away the memory of the hurt, the neglect. Then let the sun come out and fill the sky with rainbows. Let the warmth of the sun heal us wherever we are broken. Let it burn away the fog so that we can see beyond labels, beyond accents, gender or skin colour. Let the warmth and brightness of the sun melt our selfishness. So that we can share the joys and feel the sorrows of our neighbours. And let the light of the sun be so strong that we will see all people as our neighbours. Let the earth, nourished by rain; bring forth flowers to surround us with beauty. And let the mountains teach our hearts to reach upward to heaven.'

THOUGHT OF THE WEEK

Think of someone you have falling out with or haven't forgiven over something which happened in your past. Now ask yourself: 'Am I going to bring this grudge to the grave?'

THIRTEEN

RANDOM ACTS OF LOVE AND KINDNESS

Sometimes people come into our lives and we know right away that they were meant to be there, to serve some purpose, whether it is to teach us a lesson or to help us figure out who we are or who we want to become. Sometimes things happen to us that seem horrible, painful or unfair, but on reflection we find that without overcoming those obstacles we would never have realised our potential. The people we meet affect our lives, the success and downfalls we experience help to create who we are and who we become. The following story might help to explain what I am thinking.

This young man was driving home one evening, on the old Loughrea to Galway road. Work in his community was almost as slow as his beat-up Ford Focus but he never quit looking. Ever since the factory closed, he'd been unemployed and with winter coming on, the chill had finally hit home.

It was a lonely road since the new motorway had been built. It was starting to get dark and light rain was coming down. He'd better get a move on. You know, he almost didn't see the old lady, stranded on the side of the road. But even in the dusk, he could see she needed help. So he pulled up in front of her Mercedes and got out.

Even with the smile on his face, she was worried. No one had stopped to help, for the previous hour or so. Was he going to hurt her? He didn't look safe. He looked poor and hungry. He could see that she was frightened, standing out there in the cold. He knew how she felt. It was that chill which only fear can put in you. He said, "I'm here to help you. You wait in the car where it's warm? By the way, my name is Fearghal."

Well, all she had was a flat tyre, but for an old lady that was bad enough. Fearghal crawled under the car looking for a place to put the jack, skinning his knuckles a time or two. Soon he was able to change the tyre. As he was tightening up the lug nuts, she rolled down the window and began to talk to him. She told him that she was from Dublin and was only just passing through. She couldn't thank him enough for coming to her aid. Fearghal just smiled as he closed her boot. She asked him how much she owed him. Any amount would have been all right with her. She had already imagined all the awful things that could have happened had he not stopped. Fearghal didn't think twice about the money. This was not a job to him. This was helping someone in need, and God knows there were plenty who had given him a hand in the past.

He had lived his whole life that way and it never occurred to him to act any other way. He told her if she really wanted to pay him back, the next time she saw someone who needed help, she could give that person the assistance that they needed, and Fearghal added "...and you can think of me."

He waited until she started her car and drove off. It had been a cold and depressing day, but he felt good as he headed for home, disappearing into the twilight.

A few miles down the road the lady saw the lights of a small cafe. She went in to grab a bite to eat and warm up before she made the last leg of her trip home.

The waitress came over and brought a clean towel to wipe her wet hair. She had a sweet smile, even though she had been on her feet for the whole day. The lady noticed that the waitress was heavily pregnant but she didn't let the strain and aches change her attitude. The old lady wondered how someone who had so little could be so giving to a stranger.

Then she remembered Fearghal...

After the lady finished her meal, and the waitress went to get change for a €100 note, the lady slipped right out the door. She was gone by the time the waitress came back. She wondered where the lady could be, then she noticed something written on the napkin under which were four €100 notes. There were tears in her eyes when she read what the lady wrote. It said: "You don't owe me anything, I have been there too. Somebody once helped me out the way I'm helping you. If you really want to pay me back, here is what you do: Do not let this chain of love end with you."

Well, there were tables to clear, sugar bowls to fill, and people to serve but the waitress made it through another day. That night when she got home from work and climbed into bed, she was thinking about the money and what the lady had written. How could the lady have known how much she and her husband needed it? With the baby due the following month, it was going to be hard. She knew how worried her husband was, and as he lay sleeping next to her, she gave him a soft kiss and whispered soft and low, "Everything's gonna be all right – I love you, Fearghal."

A MOMENT IN TIME

Try practising random acts of love and kindness and if you are the beneficiary of a loving or kind act why not pass it on. We are never prepared for what we receive.

TIME OUT

FOURTEEN

SEEKING SERENITY

'God grant me the serenity to accept the things I cannot change, courage to change the things I can, and wisdom to know the difference.'

Acceptance is the key to the Serenity Prayer, commonly recited at 12 steps addiction group meetings. If we can understand what this prayer means then we can better understand what recovery from addiction and worry is about. As humans we have two basic strategies for handling any situation that disturbs us. One is to change the situation. For example, if we are short of a few bob, we can trim our latte or cream bun allowance or seek an increase in our weekly pay. If we are lonely we can call a loved one. This is how we usually cope with our anguish and distress. We try to alter the world outside us. And in many cases, this is powerful and appropriate.

However, circumstances are sometimes beyond our power. A sudden unpredictable expense might destroy our plans to save money. We can call a friend or a loved one to suppress our loneliness but that person may not be at home. Hoping we can control every event that comes our way is like hoping we can control the weather or how many points Joe Canning scores for Galway.

In such moments, we often forget we have a second option. We can change our response to the situation. Viktor Frankl was prisoner number 119104 in a concentration camp in the Second World War. He spent most of his time alone, laying tracks for railway lines. Most people assume he would have been miserable or gone insane, but even in the concentration camp, Frankl felt free.

In his book, 'Man's Search For Meaning', he concluded that everything can be taken from us except our ability to choose our attitude in any given set of circumstances. Another name for this freedom is acceptance. And acceptance is the key to the Serenity Prayer.

Frankl discovered this second option while he was in the concentration camp. Escape was not feasible; he was powerless over the situation. So he responded by dwelling on thoughts that empowered him. More specifically, Frankl stayed alive to the beauty of nature. Even the Nazis could not take away sunsets. He imagined amusing incidents that could take place in the future, allowing him to laugh. And he remembered the people he loved. He wrote how a man who has nothing left in the world may still know bliss, if only for a brief moment, in the contemplation of the people and things he loved and in the good he did in his life.

Complete this sentence: 'I would be happy if I had...' Typical answers include the right job, the right relationship, a new car, a child, a house. All of these have to do with the first option, having the right circumstances. All are attempts to change the world outside our heads.

For example, addiction is something we are powerless over and recovery from addiction means looking for serenity elsewhere – in the world inside our heads. Recovery hinges on learning to dwell on beliefs, attitudes and thoughts that remain true no matter what happens to us. The most important thing to learn and remember is that there is always another way of looking at anything.

The Serenity Prayer reminds us that we should change what we can, accept that which we cannot change and strive to know the difference. For people in recovery, for all of us, such knowledge is the heart of serenity. The Serenity Prayer offers us more than an insightful look back at our past; it provides us with a road map for our future. Dreams do come true if you take the time to think about what you want in life. Get to know yourself. Be honest with yourself. Always believe in yourself. Find out what you are good at. Don't be afraid to make mistakes. Work hard to achieve success. Don't give up; just try harder. Dare to dream and then try to achieve them.

A MOMENT IN TIME

Pray for people you know with addiction that they will say the Serenity Prayer and use it as a road map for their future so that they will have the courage and wisdom to use it in their future dealings with others.

TIME OUT

FIFTEEN

CHERISHING YOUR LIFE

One day I was on my way to meet a friend on the prom at Salthill. The prom is about 20 minute walk from my house. On the way as I listened to my radio the news broke of the terrible atrocity in Norway where over 80 people lost their lives. Also in the headlines was the story about people dying of hunger in the horn of Africa.

Closer to home one of my dearest friends was waiting in vigil with family members at the bedside of a close family member. But they were thankful for her life and this special time that they had with her. I titled this thought 'Cherishing your life,' because in that short time of walking from my house to the prom I was reminded of how much can change for any one of us in a moment.

We sometimes get so caught up in our routines and in the business of living that we take it for granted that we will be here tomorrow or next week or next year. We put things off – little but important things like spending time over a cup of tea with a friend; writing e-mails or making phone calls to family members who live far away; thanking people of all ages who do nice things for us; appreciating the blooming flowers and the nurturing of nature that lovingly supports our lives.

Sometimes, we forget how each new day is a gift to us to learn and grow and share again, to put aside the regrets of yesterday and move forward with a renewed spirit for living and loving more fully. For all we know, today – this moment – is all we really have. Many people nowadays don't know how to hold on to 'today.' They don't cherish the opportunities right in front of them but worry about the future. No matter what, all people can have are today and this moment. A story from the eastern philosophers my might help to explain.

❀ ❀ ❀

'In ancient times, there was a little monk who took care of the yard at the temple. Every morning he had to get up early to sweep the leaves and that was the only thing that required his effort. That was not an easy job, particularly between autumn and winter with a huge amount of leaves flying all over the yard. It took him quite a bit of time to clear the leaves every day. Consequently, he wanted to find a way to make his life easier. Later another monk in the temple who considered himself bright told the little monk: "Why don't you shake the tree really hard before you sweep tomorrow and all the leaves will fall down, then you only need to sweep once. The little monk was very excited and thought what a permanent solution that was.

The following day, the little monk got up early and shook every tree hard. He thought that he could sweep all the leaves in one day and that would be it. However, the next morning, he found out that there were just as many leaves in the yard as before. He was depressed that he had to work hard again. Then the abbot came over and saw him being unhappy. After hearing the story, the abbot said: "Foolish child, no matter how hard you shake the trees today, the leaves that are supposed to fall tomorrow will still fall tomorrow."

Everything as they say under the sun has been pre-arranged and there is a season for everything and no one can hurry things up. Truly managing today well is the correct attitude toward life. There is no need to wait for tomorrow because tomorrow consists of a lot of uncertainty. No one knows for sure what will happen in the environment around them or how it will change. It will be hard to predict or even to understand.

When you are wholeheartedly waiting for tomorrow, you

are wasting today. Giving up today is giving up your best opportunity. Only today is real and valid. In the journey of life, tomorrow seems pale and dim compared to today. Today, you can heal your wound, wipe off your tears, and fulfil your dreams from yesterday. Holding on to today, you have mastered the secret of time. Cherishing today is cherishing your life.

A MOMENT IN TIME

In the wake of all the tragedies, I send out this loving invitation that I read recently in a book by Chris Durring. "Make this present moment count. Spend your time this week thoughtfully on words and actions that serve you and others well."

TIME OUT

SIXTEEN

THE POWER IN WORDS OF ENCOURAGEMENT

Sometimes the smallest gesture or word of encouragement can make a huge impact on someone's life. There are many different ways we can show kindness and encouragement to others. A smile, a door being held open, a handwritten note, a kind word of encouragement or just helping someone pick up something that has fallen. It's not the size of the action or the word of encouragement that is important but the difference that a small action or word of encouragement makes. As usual a story might help explain.

A group of frogs were travelling through the woods and two of them fell into a deep pit. All the other frogs gathered around the pit. When they saw how deep the pit was, they told the two frogs that they were as good as dead. The two frogs ignored the comments and tried to jump up out of the pit with all of their might. The other frogs kept telling them to stop, that there was no hope. Finally, one of the frogs took heed to what the other frogs were saying and gave up. He slowly fell away.

The other frog continued to jump as hard as he could. Once again, the crowd of frogs yelled at him to stop the pain and give up. He jumped even harder and finally made it out. When he got out, the other frogs said, "Did you not hear us?" The frog explained to them that he was deaf. He thought they were encouraging him the entire time.

This story teaches two lessons: There is power of life and death in our words. An encouraging word to someone who is down can lift them up and help them make it through the day. A destructive word to someone who is down can be what it takes to make them feel even worse. Be careful of what you say. Speak life to those who cross your path. The power of words can have such an effect on someone for good or for bad. It is sometimes hard to understand that an encouraging word can go such a long way. Anyone can speak words that tend to rob another of the spirit to continue in difficult times. But it takes someone special who will take the time to encourage another. Be special to others as much as you can!

A MOMENT IN TIME

Never underestimate the power of your words or actions. God puts us in each other's lives to impact on one another in some way. Always look for the good in others and remember a little word of encouragement can go a long way and that it has the capacity to actually change the course of another human being's life.

SEVENTEEN

HOW TO MAKE A DIFFERENCE

Many people believe that they don't have what it takes to make a difference to the world they live in. The truth is, everyone is put in this world to contribute and make a difference in our own unique way. It just needs to be something you do with the intention of 'doing good'. As Mother Teresa once said, "If you can't feed 100 people, then feed just one." You already have what it takes to make the world a better place. The size of the contribution is not what matters most. The key here is to have the heart to do it. Little efforts count, and you can start making small contributions today. There is a saying that goes as follows: "Nobody can do everything, but everyone can do something." If you think that everything has been taken care of by somebody and your contribution is not going to make much of a difference, then you're wrong. Can you imagine if everyone else starts to think the same way?

In fact, it is our responsibility to seek ways to contribute, large and small. You don't have to be concerned you're only capable of making small contributions. What counts is the effort. Remember that hundreds of candles can be lit from a single candle and the life of the candle will not be shortened. Happiness never decreases by being shared. Happiness and love are the two greatest gifts you can give to the world.

So often, we're too indulged in our own gratifications that we forget there are people in our world who we can make a little happier. As the saying goes: "To receive, you must first give." The more you give, the more you'll receive. Let us remind ourselves that in order to receive more happiness and love, we need to spread more first. There is no better thing that you can do in life than to love someone or care for someone. Start doing whatever is within your ability today. Start showing more concern and love to the people around you. Every effort counts, no matter how small and insignificant it may seem. Just do something and do something good.

Remember that everybody has something to offer. Indeed, most of us have many things to offer and, in a lot of cases, special expertise is not required. We are all capable of giving that which people need most of all now in our county and world: LOVE.

Love translates into time, service and the sharing of oneself. The whole meaning of our lives is bound up with love. We find happiness in loving others and being loved in return. All our experiences of love are experiences of God. And what really brings God's love home to us and makes it real is the love of another human being. Then we feel it and know it. After all, it is love that heals us, encourages us, frees us, makes us grow and it is love that makes life meaningful. You see all of us have the capacity, some more than others, to help the needy and treat them with love, compassion and respect and show them that there are people in our county and world willing to help them. As usual I will finish up with a story that we all might have heard before written by some anonymous mystic many moons ago.

'Once upon a time there was a wise man who used to go to the ocean to do his writing. He had a habit of walking the beach before he began his work. One day as he looked down the beach, he saw a human figure moving like a dancer. As he got closer, he saw that it was a young man who wasn't dancing, but instead was reaching down to the beach, picking up something and very gently throwing it into the ocean.

As he got closer he called out: 'Good morning. What are you doing?'

The young man paused, looked up and replied, 'Throwing starfish into the ocean.'

'Why are you doing that as the sun is up and the tide is going out.'

'If I don't throw them in they'll die,' said the stranger.

'Don't you realise that there are miles and miles of beach and starfish all along it. You can't possibly make a difference.'

The young man listened politely. Then he bent down, picked up another starfish and threw it into the sea, past the breaking waves and said: 'It made a difference for that one.'

There is something very special in each and every one of us. We've all been gifted the ability to make a difference. And if we can become aware of that gift, we gain the power to shape the future. We must each find our starfish. And if we throw our stars wisely and well, the world will be blessed.

A MOMENT IN TIME
See how you can make a difference for the good in people's lives and seek out family, friends, charity or community organisations that might need your help and support.

TIME OUT

EIGHTEEN

CHILDREN MUST HAVE HOPE

Events have happened lately that gives a person pause to wonder about what life is really all about. The sadness that has happened to children and youth in Norway and Somalia and in many parts of Africa and indeed the children who suffered in Cloyne and other dioceses in Ireland and who died in state care in Ireland is unbearable to contemplate.

When I was in Ethiopia adopting our second little girl a few years ago, there was so much tragedy and suffering everywhere I went. The people, especially the children in these areas need plenty of our help, support, love and prayers.

To live without hope is the most crushing of all burdens. Everywhere I have travelled over the last 20 years in the developing world especially in famine torn areas I've seen children with a look of despair. It reminded me of the words of the US writer James Agee, who said: ' In every child who is born, no matter what circumstances, the potentiality of the human race is also born again...and in each of us is born again our terrific responsibility towards human life.'

After seeing the recent events where there was so much needless loss of life I have started to hug my two little girls more tightly each day and I am constantly thanking God for giving me the opportunity to have them in our lives and for the wonderful gift they are to my wife and myself. I remember the poem called 'To my Child' on the wall of a children's hospice that I visited:

TO MY CHILD

Just for this morning, I am going to smile when I see your face and laugh when I feel like crying.

Just for this morning, I will let you choose what you want to wear, and smile and say how perfect it is.

Just for this morning, I am going to step over the washing, and pick you up and take you to the park and play.

Just for this morning, I will leave the dishes in the sink, and let you teach me how to put that puzzle of yours together.

Just for this afternoon, I will unplug the telephone and keep the computer off, and sit with you in the backyard and blow bubbles.

Just for this afternoon, I will not yell once, not even a tiny grumble when you scream and whine for the ice-cream truck, and I will buy you one if he comes by.

Just for this afternoon, I won't worry about what you are going to be when you grow up, or second-guess every decision I have made where you are concerned.

Just for this afternoon, I will let you help me bake cakes, and I won't stand over you trying to fix them.

Just for this afternoon, I will take us to Supermac's and buy us both a Supermac's meal so we can have both toys.

Just for this evening, I will hold you in my arms and tell you a story about how you were born and how much I love you.

Just for this evening, I will let you splash in the bath and not get angry.

Just for this evening, I will let you stay up late while we sit on the porch and count all the stars.

Just for this evening, I will snuggle beside you for hours, and miss my favourite TV shows.

Just for this evening, when I run my fingers through your hair as you pray, I will simply be grateful that God has given me the greatest gift ever given.

I will think about the mothers and fathers who are searching for their missing children, the mothers and fathers who are visiting their children's graves instead of their bedrooms, and mothers and fathers who are in hospital rooms watching their children suffer senselessly and screaming inside that they can't handle it anymore. And when I kiss you good night, I will hold you a little tighter, a little longer. It is then, that I will thank God for you, and ask him for nothing, except one more day...

A MOMENT IN TIME

Do something special with your loved ones, especially your children because life is short and we must give them real hope for the future for they are our future. Please remember all the children who need your help, support and prayers now, for tomorrow will be too late for a lot of them.

TIME OUT

NINETEEN

SMILE A WHILE

'Smiley' is the nickname I call my wife Jacqui, who is my best friend. Every time I meet her, before ever a word is spoken, I know she is glad to see me and that she cares about me. Why? Because of the beautiful radiance of her smile.

For me, one of the ways I sense spirituality in humans is by smiling. Smiles spell love, compassion, generosity, kindness, warmth, reliability, patience and real-love.

'God's love' is not just romantic love, it's much more than that, it is a never-ending series of positive, creative, affirming, challenging, forgiving, healing and protecting feelings and actions whose purposes are to promote our sense of well-being for ourselves and others and help's us to be aware of how God feels lovingly and warmly towards us.

A smile is a part of that purpose and is a powerful means of communication. It is made up, not only of parted lips, but also of eyes, which sparkle or weep, eyes, which are full of tenderness, acceptance, humour, forgiveness, love and compassion.

Many people speak the language of smiles, especially children. I remember the smiles on orphaned and abandoned children in Africa and India and the unspoken words of love and appreciation in their smiles is a memory I will never forget.

Smiles transform the faces of all people, giving them charm, grace and a beautiful radiance. Such smiles portray the presence of love. They pour into others a portion of that love. Love changes people and it encourages them.

There is a saying that goes: 'A smile costs nothing, but gives much. It enriches those who receive it, without making poorer those who give. It takes but a moment, but the memory of it lasts forever. It brings rest to the weary, cheer to those who are discouraged, sunshine to the sad and it is nature's best antidote for trouble, for it is something that is of no value to anyone until it is given away. Some people are too tired to give you a smile. Give them one of yours, as no one needs a smile so much as he who has no more to give.'

It is often said and I agree that smiling is infectious, you catch it like the 'flu, when someone smiled at me today, I started smiling too. I passed around the corner and someone saw my grin. When he smiled, I realised I'd passed it on to him. I thought about that smile then I realised its worth. A single smile, just like mine could travel round the earth. So, if you feel a smile begin, don't leave it undetected. Let's start an epidemic quick, and get the world infected.

A MOMENT IN TIME

See what your smile does for you. You might find that you should smile more often and that the power of a smile will work wonders for you and for others.

TWENTY

THE SECRET OF BEING THANKFUL

It's hard to be thankful for anything when it seems that everything is going wrong in your world and I'm not talking about the fact that the bottom has fallen out of the economy. I'm thinking about when you have one of those days when your child is sick, the washing machine has just spewed soapy water all over the place, and to top it off, your car won't start.

The last thing you want to do is say thank you for any of this. But, there are reasons to be thankful in our lives. First of all, be thankful that your child is at home sick, and not in the hospital. Be thankful that you have such things as a washing machine and a car. There are many out there who don't have these luxuries.

Even when things seem totally lost, there are several reasons to be thankful. There are a lot of people out there who believe that special occasions are the only time to sit down and count their blessings. I believe that everyday is a reason to be thankful. Instead of complaining about having to go to work, be thankful that you have a job and can take care of your family.

Think about all the people out there who can't work or those that have lost their jobs due to downsizing and the effects of the economy going bust. You have a lot of reasons to be thankful for, if you just take the time to look for them. It's easy to sit around and grumble about the way your life is going. However, finding the silver lining can be the difference between having a bad day and having a great day. It can take a bit of creative thinking but if you look deeply enough, there are some positive points to focus on. Sometimes these points may seem trivial but a positive outlook will make being thankful much easier.

Take a look at some of the things going on in your life. For everything you see as being a disappointment or a reason to complain, see if you can come up with something to be thankful for. We, as a society, have forgotten that it's the little things in life that make it worth living. We forget that generations before us had it much worse than we do now, and they almost always found reasons to be thankful.

They were grateful that they had food to give their families, that they had a piece of land in which to build their homes and that they had the ability to get out of bed each morning. Remember, no matter how bad your life seems, there is at least one reason to give thanks. Take a moment to look over your situation and see if you can find that one positive aspect and embrace it. When you have a positive outlook and a reason to be thankful, others around you will pick up on this. It could eventually give everyone else a reason to be thankful.

Work hard at what you like to do and try to overcome all obstacles. Laugh at your mistakes and praise yourself for learning from them. Pick some flowers and appreciate the beauty of nature. Say hello to strangers and enjoy the people you know. Don't be afraid to show your emotions, laughing and crying make you feel better. Love your friends and family, they are the most important part of your life.

Feel the calmness on a quiet sunny day. Look for a rainbow and always remember life is better than it seems. You must feel confident enough within yourself to follow your own dreams. You must be willing to make sacrifices. You must be capable of changing and rearranging your priorities so that your final goal can be achieved. Sometimes, familiarity and comfort need to be challenged. There are times when you must take a few extra chances and create your own realities. Be strong enough to at least try to make your life better.

Be confident enough that you won't settle for a compromise just to get by. Appreciate yourself by allowing yourself the opportunities to grow, develop and find your true sense of purpose. Don't stand in someone else's shadow when it's your sunlight that should lead the way.

A MOMENT IN TIME

Be thankful that you don't already have everything you desire. If you did, what would there be to look forward to? Be thankful when you don't know something, as it gives you the opportunity to learn. Be thankful for the difficult times. During those times you grow. Be thankful for your limitations, because they give you opportunities for improvement.

TIME OUT

TWENTY-ONE

HELP SOMEONE TODAY

None of us can help everyone, but each of us can help someone near us. It may be only a smile, an encouraging word, a shoulder to cry on, or a hug to motivate them. Sometimes, it takes more. Figuratively speaking, it might require a swift kick in the behind or a warning of what the future could hold, if attitudes and actions aren't changed. We need to be honest in our assessments. Remember, every person you see today is someone who God loves. Doesn't that presume that people should see in us a love expressed through our deeds and interactions with others? The essence of God's kingdom is unselfish love. When God's love is present, it results in us helping others. A famous story of neighbourliness from olden days will help me explain the good results you can receive from helping others.

'Once there was a farmer who grew award-winning corn. Each year he entered his corn in the farming awards event where it won a blue ribbon. One year a newspaper reporter interviewed him and learned something interesting about how he grew it. The reporter discovered that the farmer shared his seed corn with his neighbours.

"How can you afford to share your best seed corn with your neighbours when they are entering corn in competition with yours each year?" the reporter asked.

"The winds pick up pollen from the ripening corn and swirls it from field to field. If my neighbours grow inferior corn, cross-pollination will steadily degrade the quality of my corn. If I am to grow good corn, I must help my neighbours grow good corn." He is very much aware of the connectedness of life. His corn cannot improve unless that of others also improves.

So it is with our lives. Those who choose to live in peace must help their neighbours to live in peace. Those who choose to live well must help others to live well, for the value of a life is measured by the lives it touches. And those who choose to be happy must help others to find happiness, for the welfare of each is bound up with the welfare of all. The lesson for each of us is this: If we are to grow good corn we must help our neighbour grow good corn.

A MOMENT IN TIME

There is a certain gratification in worldly accomplishments, but it doesn't bring the satisfaction and fulfilment we crave in our hearts. When you become a giver instead of a taker, a helper instead of a receiver, you will find comfort, contentment, and joy in your living.

TWENTY-TWO

BE PREPARED FOR IT TO GET BETTER

The following story was told to me by a friend who was saying a station mass in my house a few years ago.

A woman, who had been diagnosed with a terminal illness and given three months to live contacted her priest so that she might get her things in order. Duly, he came to her house to discuss certain aspects of her final wishes. She told him which songs she wanted sung at her funeral, what scriptures she would like read, and what outfits she wanted to be buried in. The woman also requested to be buried with her favourite bible. Everything was in order and the priest was preparing to leave when the woman suddenly remembered something very important to her.

'There is one more thing,' she said excitedly.

'What's that?' the priest replied.

'This is very important,' she said, 'I want to be buried with a fork in my right hand.

The priest stood looking at the woman, not knowing quite what to say. 'That surprises you, doesn't it?' the woman asked. The priest nodded.

The woman explained: 'In all my years of attending socials and gala dinners, I always remember that when the dishes of the main course were been cleared, someone would inevitably lean over and say, "Keep your fork". It was my favourite part because I knew that something better was coming, like Goya's velvety chocolate cake or Griffin's Bakery deep dish apple pie or one of the Malt House Restaurant scrumptious desserts.

Something wonderful, and with substance.

I just want people to see me there in that coffin with a fork in my hand and I want them to wonder: "What's the fork for?" Then I want you to tell them: "Keep your fork, the best is yet to come."

The priest's eyes welled up with tears of joy as he hugged the woman goodbye. He knew this would be one of the last times he would see her before her death. But he also knew that the woman had a better grasp of heaven than he did. She knew that something better was coming.

As people were paying their respects by her coffin, they noticed the pretty dress she had asked to be laid out in, they noticed that she was clasping her favourite bible, and then they noticed the fork in her right hand.

Over and over, the priest heard the question, 'What's the fork for?' And over and over he smiled.

During his homily, the priest told the people of the conversation he had with the woman shortly before she died. He told them about the fork and what it symbolised to her. He told them he would never forget the woman and that he felt they would remember her too. He was right.

A MOMENT IN TIME
The next time you reach down for your fork remember to be prepared – something better is on the way.

TWENTY-THREE

IT'S ALL ABOUT THE JOURNEY

Recently, I ran a marathon in the North Pole thanks to the generosity of my great friend Ritchie Donovan, one of the world's great Ultra Marathon runners. For anyone unfamiliar with the marathon distance, it's 26.2 miles, and a really long way to run and seems even longer when you're running it on snow at minus 35 degrees.

Though the marathon might be considered just an athletic event by some, from my experience over that weekend I would refer to it as a metaphor for life.

Running a marathon reinforces the idea that in life, it's about the journey, not the end result. As I ran, I realised that this might be the only time that I would ever run a marathon, so I needed to savour the experience. I thought: "This is it, the moment I have worked so hard for."

I needed to enjoy the marathon experience, not wish it away and especially because it was at the North Pole and what an experience it was with many epiphanies and spiritual moments at the top of the world.

Often we wish our lives away, wanting to reach a certain place in life to be happy. However, the satisfaction derived from setting an objective is not so much in attaining it as in the anticipation and striving toward the end goal. So, try to enjoy the journey as much as the end results as I did with my North Pole marathon attempt.

Running a marathon is as much a mental challenge as a physical one. Yes, there is intense hard work that must be done to be physically prepared but when the later miles arrive, and your legs begin to complain, it's up to the mind to override the urge to quit.

You must figure out some mental techniques to apply whether that's dividing the race into sections, doing each mile for someone's intentions or a loved one in your life.

I did that with my run in the North Pole and by chatting with others along the way I managed to enjoy the journey all the way.

Similar strategies can be applied to everyday life. We may face difficult situations that require mental toughness, but we can make it through if we just find the strength to keep going.

Everyone needs a challenge in life. Too much difficulty can result in frustration, but so can a lack of challenge. Challenge is necessary for a person's spirit to emerge. It is a state achieved when a person is completely absorbed in an activity. Achieving this spirit involves a delicate balance between the difficulty of the task at hand and the skill of the person working on it.

Achieving this spirit from within regularly seems to be one element of being a happy person, and to experience this spirit it's necessary to be part of a learning experience that requires focus and concentration. At the North Pole I am sure I found that spirit.

I was amazed at the rush of energy I got while running the last stretch of my marathon. I thought my legs had given me all the energy they had left, but in the last mile I picked up my speed and gave it all I had and happily and emotionally crossed the finishing line with my Galway and Offaly flags waving uncontrollably.

In a marathon, as in life, the key is just to keep going, even if that means going slowly. No matter how hard things get, there is usually an end in sight, if we just keep going forward. We get steered off course and put all our energy toward things that ultimately – when it really gets down to it – don't matter much at all. Remembering what really matters in life requires a conscious effort, and here's to each of us trying to live a life that really matters and that always helps rather than hurts our fellow human beings.

A MOMENT IN TIME

Keep going no matter what challenges life throws at you and don't be afraid to give help and receive help as you make that journey through life and don't forget to savour the experience as it is all about the journey and not the end result.

TIME OUT

TWENTY-FOUR

COURAGE TO TAKE ACTION

I was watching Spiderman the movie recently and the song of the film was 'A hero can save us'. It got me thinking about who are our world heroes at present with unemployment, rising household costs, poverty, suicide, bullying, conflicts and so many financial uncertainties.

I've always been a fan of superhero movies and comics. The obsession started young when my friends and I would pretend we were superheroes – dressing up in costumes and imagining we had special powers. Actually one of my friends donned the Superman outfit on a recent charity cycle from Maynooth to Galway to raise much needed funds for Down Syndrome Ireland and in some ways it reminded me of my childhood.

In my mind's eye of watching those old films, the team-ups among superheroes were always the most exciting. Often, some misunderstanding would put them against one another but then they would unite against a common threat – the super villains. Earth's mightiest superheroes would only come together when it took such super-collaboration to do the impossible.

The G8 is kind of like Earth's mightiest heroes in the real world or so we'd like to think. These leaders – presidents and prime ministers have been given special powers through the votes and confidence of the world's most developed countries. We look to them to help lead and guide us. And once a year, they gather to collaborate with one another. We have many villains in the world, who decide on issues that affect our lives. They have an even larger impact on those living in extreme poverty, the one billion living in hunger and the nearly five million children who die from hunger-related causes every year.

Lots of Irish organisations such as Self Help Africa, Alan Kerin's Projects, Trocaire, GOAL, Concern and many more are asking our leaders to show global leadership by joining together to co-ordinate achievable and sustainable solutions that include nutritious, affordable, locally-grown food for those living with hunger in our world.

It seems impossible but if each of us does our part, we could live in a hunger-free world. It starts with each of us and we have to show our leaders this is important to us. My own daughter, Mia, came home recently from an Easter camp after making a pizza and a cake and wanted me to bring them to Africa to feed the malnourished children. Children can speak the truth so profoundly at times. This spurred me to do something specific for World Food Day.

A MOMENT IN TIME

We all have a decision to make in life. Will we be passive spectators or are we going to become a vital part of the world transformation that is needed? Without the courage to take action, our beliefs will merely turn to idle thoughts or the famous but highly useless 'good intentions'.

TWENTY-FIVE

BELIEVE IN YOURSELF

A few years ago I was sitting on a beautiful white and red couch in RTE studios on the set of the revisit of Operation Transformation six months after I had taken part in it. I was asked a question from one of the show's experts about what got me to where I was and I answered: 'Self belief'.

There are times when we believe in everything and everybody but ourselves. There is a constant search for mentors and role models when they exist within us. The most brutal hardship that we take is the one that we inflict upon ourselves. We make one mistake and using a boxing analogy we count ourselves out.

Depression is a dark and dreary place where we drink tears for breakfast, lunch and dinner. We tend to use our carnal mind, eyes and ears that are distorted during this dark time. There may be days when you get up in the morning and things aren't the way you had hoped they would be. That's when you have to tell yourself that things will get better.

There are times when people disappoint you and let you down but those are the times when you must remind yourself to trust your own judgments and opinions and to keep your life focused on believing in yourself. There will be challenges to face and changes to make in your life and it is up to you to accept them. Constantly keep yourself headed in the right direction. It may not be easy at times, but in the end you will find a stronger sense of who you are. So when the days come that are filled with frustration and unexpected responsibilities, remember to believe in yourself and all you want your life to be, because the challenges and changes will only help you to find the goals that you know are meant to come true for you.

Sometimes people come into your life and you know right away that they were meant to be there. To serve some sort of purpose, teach you a lesson or help figure out who you are or who you want to become. I think Operation Transformation was one of those experiences for me where I met four other fantastic leaders and experts and class behind-the-scenes people. You never know who these people may be but when you lock eyes with them, you know that they will affect your life in some profound way.

Everything happens for a reason. Illness, injury, love, lost moments of true greatness and sheer stupidity all occur to test the limits of your soul. Without these small tests, life would be like a smoothly-paved, straight, flat road to nowhere. Safe and comfortable but dull and utterly pointless. The people you meet affect your life. The successes and downfalls that you experience can create who you are and the bad experiences can be good teachers. In fact, they are probably the most poignant and important ones. If someone hurts you, betrays you or breaks your heart, forgive them because they have helped you to learn who to trust and who to be cautious in trusting.

Make every day count. Appreciate every moment and take from it everything that you possibly can, for you may never be able to experience it again. Talk to people you have never talked to before – and actually listen. Let yourself fall in love, break free and set your sights high. Tell yourself you are a great individual and believe in yourself, for if you don't believe in yourself, no one else will believe in you. Create your own life and then go out and live it. "If you take your eyes off your goals, all you see are obstacles."

A MOMENT IN TIME
Revisit your life's lessons and see what you are doing about them and then go out and live them and believe in yourself.

TWENTY-SIX

SYMBOLS OF TRUE LOVE AND CARE

I wrote a heart-wrenching A Moment In Time to coincide with Mother's Day some time ago. It was about the love a Japanese mother had for her baby daughter during the earthquake there happened and the way she sacrificed her life to safe her. Now I want to share with your the real life story of a father and child who died in a house fire here in Ireland.

Anthony, his wife Kelly and wee Nadine woke with smoke filling their house, they could not get down the stairs because of the flames, but managed to reach the bedroom window. Anthony sat his daughter on the window-sill while he helped his wife out the window doing his best to lower her as far as he could. He then reached for his daughter but she was gone. In the chaos she must have become confused and left the sill. Anthony stumbled and raced through the house and eventually found her, but at that point it was too late to get back to the window. He did his best carefully cradling his daughter in his arms protecting her from the flames. Tragically they both died in the blaze. Nadine was found still cradled in his arms without a mark on her.

"There was just no way he would have left without her," Nadine's aunt explained. "He saved his wife and tried to save his daughter, protecting her right to the end." They were both buried in the one coffin wrapped in each other's arms.

There is something about a father or a mother protecting their child that is just deeply moving. I think dads and moms everywhere hope that they would act with this kind of courage to protect those entrusted to their care. I think every woman hopes that her man and every man hopes that his woman would show this kind of selflessness. I think every child carries the belief that their dad and mam are brave and smart and well able to step in and solve their problems.

These kinds of hopes, instincts, and beliefs just seem to be a part of the human make-up. The ancient stories from every culture attest to the universality of such traits. Bravery, commitment to duty, and sacrificial love are given a place of honour amongst all peoples. These kinds of hopes, instincts, and beliefs remind us that life is ultimately about a mission to complete, a duty to fulfil, a calling to live up to.

A MOMENT IN TIME

Make your children feel the most special they can be and show them how much they mean to you in how you care about and love them. Most of all let them know that your love for them is not just for today or tomorrow but for all time.

TWENTY-SEVEN

WAYS OF LIVING A HAPPY LIFE

How we achieve a happy life is different for each one of us. Our expectations, life experiences, passions and even our personalities all contribute to the level of happiness we experience in our lives. Some find happiness in their careers while others prefer the happiness found in their sports, their religion and spirituality, their reading and writing, or their relationships.

No matter how you define happiness for yourself, there are various ways to bring and sustain more happiness into your life. The following ways to live a happy life can be tailored to fit your needs. Over time, these strategies will become positive habits that will begin to bring more happiness into your life.

❁ ❁ ❁

Take the time to notice what is good in your life. See the glass as being half-full, rather than half-empty. Take all that life throws at you and reframe it with what's good about the situation. At the end of the day, you will be more at ease. Learn to be grateful and caring and you will be open to receive a wealth of happiness. One way to find your happiness is to remember the happy times of the child you were when you were younger and to contemplate the people and things you love in your life and the good that you have already done and would like to do in your life here on earth.

Merely watching acts of goodness and kindness creates a palpable rise in our moods and increases the desire for us to perform kind deeds as well. Goodness and kindness are indeed contagious and when we make a commitment to be good and kind to ourselves and to others we can experience new heights of happiness for our lives. Learn to spend time with your friends and make genuine friendships a priority in your life. Too often we are thinking back at events or looking ahead to the next event in our lives, not appreciating the 'present moment.'

There are times when we need to unwind, distress or just "to dwell." Life comes at all of us hard and fast. Time keeps going forward at its own pace, which is not always the pace we would choose. Fatigue, stress and exhaustion may begin to settle in on us faster than we may think. The best remedy for this is indeed time to rest and to dwell. The absence of aims in our lives, or more specifically avoiding to pursue our aims, makes us feel like we are stuck and ineffective. The pursuit of aims in our personal lives, in our relationships, or with our careers, is the difference between having a mediocre life or a life full of passion and enthusiasm.

Some find meaning in religion or spirituality while others find purpose in their work or relationships. Finding your vocation may be much more than accomplishing one simple way for increasing your happiness, but having a sense of purpose can perhaps bring the greatest joy of all. Know when to say no. What gives you joy and happiness the first time may not work the second time. Too much of a good thing may begin not to feel as good if it becomes more of a routine or an expectation. Have healthy and reasonable boundaries and don't overdo it.

'Be the first to say hello. Live beneath your means. Treat everyone as you want to be treated. Never give up on anybody – miracles do happen. Forget the Joneses. Be tough minded, but tender-hearted. Be kinder than you want or have to be. Don't forget that a person's greatest emotional need is to feel appreciated. Never break a promise. Learn to be cheerful even when you don't feel it. Overnight success usually takes years of hard graft. Leave everything in better condition than you found it. Winners do what losers don't want to do.'

A MOMENT IN TIME

Never give up on anything, especially your happiness. It would be like hating roses because you got scratched once by a thorn. It's crazy to give up on all your dreams because one did not come true. Never give up on anything especially trying to live a happy life.

TIME OUT

A DAILY THANKSGIVING

Robert Louis Stevenson was so right when he wrote: "The man who forgets to be thankful has fallen asleep in life". Unfortunately, because the beauties of life are so abundant, sometimes we take them for granted.

Our minds have a capacity to notice the unusual. However, the opposite is true as well: The more often we see the things around us, even the beautiful things, the more they become invisible to us. That is why we often take for granted the beauty of this world: the flowers, the trees, the sea, the birds, the clouds – even those we love. Because we see things so often, we see them less and less. Those who live in thanksgiving daily, however, have a way of opening their eyes and seeing the wonders of this world as though seeing them for the first time.

Look around you. Notice the people you care about. Notice the fragrance of the flowers and the song of the birds. Notice and give thanks for the blue of the sky, the colour of the leaves, and the white of the clouds. Enjoy every sight, every smell, every taste and every sound. When we open our eyes and give thanks for the bountiful beauty of this life, we live in thanksgiving daily. As usual a story will help.

❈ ❈ ❈

A blind boy sat on the steps of a building with a hat by his feet. He held up a sign which read: "I am blind, please help." There were only a few coins in the hat. A man was walking by. He took a few coins from his pocket and dropped them in. He then took the sign and wrote some words. He put the sign back so that everyone who walked by would see the new words.

Soon the hat began to fill up as more people were giving money. That afternoon the man who had changed the sign came to see how things were. The boy recognised his footsteps and asked, "Were you the one who changed my sign this morning?"

"I was," the man answered.

"What did you write?"

The man said, "I wrote the truth. I just said it in a different way."

What he wrote was: "Today is a beautiful day and I cannot see it."

Do you think the first sign and second sign were saying the same thing? Of course both signs told people the boy was blind. But the first sign simply said the boy was blind. The second sign told people they were so lucky that they were not blind.

A MOMENT IN TIME

Be thankful for what you have. Be creative. Be innovative. Think differently and positively. Live life with no excuse and love with no regrets. Face your past without regret. Handle your present with confidence. Prepare for the future without fear.

TWENTY-NINE

THINGS AREN'T ALWAYS AS THEY SEEM

Two travelling angels stopped to spend the night in the home of a wealthy family. The family was rude and refused to let the angels stay in the mansion's guestroom. Instead the angels were given a space in the cold basement. As they made their bed on the hard floor, the older angel saw a hole in the wall and repaired it. When the younger angel asked why, the older angel replied, "Things aren't always what they seem".

The next night the pair came to rest at the house of a very poor, but very hospitable farmer and his wife. After sharing what little food they had the couple let the angels sleep in their bed where they could have a good night's rest. When the sun came up the next morning the angels found the farmer and his wife in tears. Their only cow, whose milk had been their sole income, lay dead in the field. The younger angel was infuriated and asked the older angel: "How could you have let this happen. The first man had everything, yet you helped him," the younger angel accused. "The second family had little but was willing to share everything, and you let their cow die."

"Things aren't always what they seem," the older angel replied.

"When we stayed in the basement of the mansion, I noticed there was gold stored in that hole in the wall. Since the owner was so obsessed with greed and unwilling to share his good fortune, I sealed the wall so he wouldn't find it. Then last night as we slept in the farmer's bed, the angel of death came for his wife. I gave him the cow instead. Things aren't always what they seem."

Sometimes this is exactly what happens when things don't

turn out the way they should. If you have faith, you just need to trust that every outcome is always to your advantage. You might not know it until some time later.

> ## A MOMENT IN TIME
> *Should you find it hard to get to sleep tonight, just remember the homeless family who has no bed to lie in. Should you notice a new grey hair in the mirror, think of the cancer patient in chemo who wishes she had hair to examine?*

THIRTY

THE JAM JAR AND THE PINT OF GUINNESS

Life can be difficult. We are pressured and stressed and pulled in many different directions. Amidst the rush and hustle of the daily grind, it can be easy to lose ourselves and forget what really matters. We get steered off-course and put all our energy toward things that ultimately don't matter much at all. Remembering what really matters in life requires a conscious effort, and it is my hope that this tale helps make that effort a little easier. Here's to living a life that really matters.

When things in your life seem almost too much to handle, when 24 hours in a day are not enough, remember the jam jar...and the pint of Guinness which is my take on a spiritual parable I heard about a jam jar and coffee.

A professor friend of mine Pat Dolan stood before his class and had some items in front of him. When the class began he picked up a very large and empty jam-jar and proceeded to fill it with golf balls. He then asked one of his students Kevin Duffy if the jar was full. He agreed that it was.

The professor then picked up a box of pebbles and poured them into the jar. He shook the jar lightly. The pebbles rolled into the open areas between the golf balls he then asked Kevin again if the jar was full. He agreed it was. The professor next picked up a box of sand and poured it into the jar. Of course, the sand filled up everything else. He asked once more if the jar was full. Kevin responded with an infamous "yes." The professor then produced a pint of Guinness from under the table and poured the entire contents into the jar, effectively filling the empty space between the sand. The students and Kevin laughed. "Now," said Professor Pat Dolan, as the laughter subsided, "I want you to recognise that this jar represents your life.

"The golf balls are the important things. Your family, your children, your faith, your health, your friends, and your favourite passions. Your life would still be full if all else was taken away. The pebbles are the other things that matter. Your job, your house and your car. The sand is everything else. The small stuff.

"If you put the sand into the jar first," he continued, "There is no room for the pebbles or the golf balls. The same goes for life. If you spend all your time and energy on the small stuff, you will never have room for the things that are important to you. Pay attention to the things that are critical to your happiness. Play with your children. Show love to all of your family. Don't hold grudges, take time to get medical check-ups, follow Operation Transformation. Take your partner out for dinner. Play another 18 or spend that Sunday in Croke Park or the Aviva Stadium or go to that fashion show. There will always be time to clean the house and take out the rubbish.

In other words take care of the golf balls first, the things that really matter. Set your priorities. The rest is just sand. Kevin, the student, raised his hand and inquired what the Guinness represented. Professor Pat Dolan smiled. "I'm glad you asked. It just goes to show you that no matter how full your life may seem, there's always room for a pint of Guinness with a friend."

Everything happens for a reason. Nothing happens by chance or by means of good or bad luck. Illness, injury, love, lost moments of true greatness and sheer stupidity all occur to test the limits of your soul. Without these small tests life would be like a smoothly paved, straight, flat road to nowhere. Make every day count. Appreciate every moment and take from it everything that you possibly can, for you may never be able to experience it again. Talk to people you've never talked to before and actually listen. Hold your head up because you have every right to. Tell yourself you are a great individual and believe in yourself, for if you don't believe in yourself, no one else will believe in you either.

A MOMENT IN TIME

Make your life anything you wish. Create your own life and then go out and live it and make sure you live a life worth living and one that's full of faith and love for your fellow human being.

TIME OUT

THIRTY-ONE

MOTHER'S DAY LOVE

The occasion of Mother's Day is extraordinary for all of us. It's a time to love, kiss and hug the most precious creation of God – your mom. For her, we will always remain the small child but this is the day to visit your mom, spend time with her and reassure her of your love and care.

Mother's Day is a great reason to honour your mother and express gratitude for all the hugs, cuddles, kisses and lullabies she has endowed upon you. Mothers bear the hardships and the joys in bringing up a child. A mother is the epitome of love, serenity and forgiveness.

Mother's Day holds great significance for all of us. It's that time of the year to let your mother know that no one loves her more than her own children. The resolution to celebrate a day dedicated to the mother was signed by US President Woodrow Wilson on May 8, 1914. Since then across the world everyone celebrates Mother's Day with joy and devotion. It's a time to be grateful to your mother for what she has done for you.

We should celebrate the weekend of Mother's Day with non-stop surprises. Socialise, lunch, feast, party and have a beautiful time on this day. Get your entire family together for a breakfast or plan a picnic, be it a brunch, garden party or barbecue. Treat your mum like a queen by presenting her with a beautiful gift. It may not be the most precious gift but must be the embodiment of your true emotions. Post a card or a gift that has an emotional meaning for them.

Mother's Day gives us a great opportunity to pamper your mother for all that she has done for you over the years. You can never repay the debts, but on Mother's Day, you can create a magical place for your mother to be delighted and fly high on love and life.

❀ ❀ ❀

When God was creating mothers, it was the sixth day of 'overtime' when the angel appeared and said: "You're doing a lot of fiddling around on this one."

God replied: "Have you read the specs on this order? She has to be completely washable, but not plastic. Have 180 moveable parts...all replaceable. Run on black coffee and leftovers. Have a lap that disappears when she stands up. A kiss that can cure anything from a broken leg to a disappointed love affair. And six pairs of hands."

The angel shook her head slowly and said. 'Six pairs of hands.... no way."

"It's not the hands that are causing me problems," God remarked, "it's the three pairs of eyes that mothers have to have."

"Is that on the standard model?" asked the angel. God nodded. One pair that sees through closed doors when she asks, "What are you kids doing in there?" when she already knows. Another in the back of her head that sees what she shouldn't but what she has to know and, of course, the one's in front that can look at a child when he or she goofs up and say: "I understand and I love you without so much as uttering a word."

"God," said the angel touching his sleeve gently, "Get some rest tomorrow...."

"I can't," said God, "I'm so close to creating something so close to myself. Already I have one who heals herself when she is sick...

can feed a family of six on very little... and can get a four year old to stand under a shower."

The angel circled the model of a mother very slowly. "It's too soft," she sighed.

"But tough!" said God excitedly. "You can imagine what this mother can do or endure."

Can it think?

"Not only can it think, but it can reason and compromise," said God.

Finally, the angel bent over and ran her finger across the cheek. "There's a leak," she pronounced. "I knew you were trying to put too much into this model."

"It's not a leak," said the Lord, "It's a tear. A tear for joy, love, kindness, sadness, empathy, disappointment, pain, loneliness, and pride."

"You are a genius," said the angel. Somberly, God said, "I didn't put it there."

A MOMENT IN TIME

Surprise your Mother with a wide assortment of gifts, goodies, personalised gifts, cards, crafts, recipes, and lots more excitement and fun. Most of all let your mother know how much you love them not just for Mother's Day but all the time.

TIME OUT

THIRTY-TWO

TO EVERYTHING THERE IS A SEASON

I walk the prom in Salthill in Galway on a regular basis and actually run it on many occasions. The prom on Salthill is what I call heaven on earth. It has become a refuge for me since I moved to Galway almost 13 years ago. Just the word, refuge, offers and then gives to each one of us a few moments in our lives to take time for retreat from our every day busy lives to think and taste the beauty of nature all around us and to slow down and enjoy nature and appreciate and love life itself.

Irish people treasure laws that preserve and keep special scenic spots for us to all to enjoy. I certainly enjoy my time walking the prom in Salthill as it gives me a chance to reflect on my life. There is a right time and a good time and each season is very special. I think all four seasons are wonderful. Seasons give each one of us variety in our lives and keeps life from being dull, boring, and mundane. We adjust and are seasonable.

"To everything there is a season, and a time to every purpose under heaven." Through this line of scripture from Ecclesiastes, we learn that there are specific seasons in our life; special times set aside by God for special purposes. Every life and season in life has intrinsic value from the cradle to the grave, even if to simply let others take stock of their own abundant blessings. For life is a time-limited, dynamic process, one that leads us from one experience to the next, always with bright anticipation for the future. As christians we embrace God's promise that He is with us through it all; that eternal life awaits all who seek Him in earnest... And for that, we are profoundly grateful.

So go on... dare to love yourself and others like there is a great light awaiting you at the end of the tunnel. For each new day is a blessed opportunity to experience the seasons of life, both joyous and challenging, as they present themselves. Let the seasons in your life evolve as they will. For there really is an appointed time for everything.

'To everything there is season, a time to be born and a time to die; a time to plant and a time to pluck what is planted; a time to kill and a time to heal; a time to break down and a time to build up; a time to weep and a time to laugh; a time to mourn and a time dance; a time to cast away stones and a time to gather stones; a time to embrace and a time to refrain from embracing; a time to gain and a time to lose; A time to keep and a time to throw away; a time to tear, and a time to sew; a time to keep silence, and a time to speak; a time to love and a time to hate; a time of war and a time of peace.' Ecclesiastes 3: 1 – 8.

A MOMENT IN TIME

Live simply, love generously. Speak kindly. Care deeply. Let the seasons in your life evolve as they will. Leave the rest to God.

WHAT IS LENT?

"There's nothing wrong with me," the man said. "But sir, you've just been in a terrible car accident. You're bleeding and have some deep bruises. There may be internal damage."

"There's nothing wrong with me," he repeated.

"At least have a doctor check you out, sir. We have an ambulance right here, it wouldn't take very long."

"I told you, there's nothing wrong with me."

Then the man walks away from the car accident. His wife picks him up and drives him home. Later he dies from internal bleeding.

What exactly is Lent? What's it all about? We find the answer as we focus on a story Jesus tells about two opposite people – one who said: "There's nothing wrong with me," and one who said: "There's everything wrong with me."

One of them represents what Lent isn't, and one of them represents what Lent is.

"Two men," Jesus said, "went up to the temple to pray – a Pharisee and a tax collector." Remember, the Pharisees were the people who lived good, clean lives. The tax collectors were people who swindled others out of their money. Both of them came to church and went to the temple to pray. "The Pharisee stood up and prayed about himself: 'God, I thank you that I am not like other men – robbers, evildoers, adulterers – or even like this tax collector. I fast twice a week and give a tenth of all I earn." Maybe you can sum up his prayer this way: "I thank you, God, that there's nothing wrong with me."

Then Jesus focuses on the tax collector in his story – the opposite of the Pharisee. He had been stealing money from people his whole life – ruining the lives of others so that he could live it up. He knew that his whole life had been a disaster. Jesus says that "the tax collector stood at a distance" – he wouldn't even walk up to the front of the temple.

"He wouldn't even look up to heaven" – he was so ashamed of his sin – "but beat his breast and said, 'God have mercy on me, a sinner.'" His prayer was the opposite of the Pharisee's, wasn't it – maybe you can sum it up this way: "God, there's everything wrong with me. Help me."

Jesus tells us that Lent is a time of self-denial, a time to give up something. But Jesus isn't concerned with you giving up chocolate or not listening to your favourite CD – he's concerned with what's going on in our hearts. Lent is a time to give up the sin of duplicity – being a Christian on Sundays, but an unbeliever on Fridays. It's a time to give up the sin of being lethargic – "someday I'll get my act together spiritually. Right now, though, I'm just too busy focusing on everything except God."

What is Lent? Lent is that man who stood in the back of the temple, looked down at the ground and prayed.

"Lord, have mercy on me, a sinner." Lent is a time for us to be like that man, to give up our sinful habits, our sinful attitudes, to stand before God and to ask him to forgive us, to wash our sins away, and to empower us to turn away from our sinful past and to live new lives that are dedicated to God and to helping and loving others.

Lent is an attitude of honesty and humility, as we confess our sins to God. But Lent is also an attitude of relief and joy, knowing that our sins have been forgiven, that our slate has been wiped clean as we seek to serve our God with our lives. These next seven weeks is a time for us to look deep into our hearts, to think about our lives and how we've been living it. If people want to temporarily give up certain things for Lent as a sign of love for God, that's fine. But what Christ is really concerned about is what's in our hearts.

A MOMENT IN TIME

Begin something to make things better for yourself and those around you. We will also see how wonderful and deep God's love is for us.

TIME OUT

THIRTY-FOUR

WISHING YOU ALL 'ENOUGH'

When we display our love and care for other people, it brings happiness into our lives. I've found in my journey so far in this life, showing love, lending a helping hand and showing I care is one of God's greatest gifts to me. If love lives within us, we can share it with our families, friends and those who are total strangers to us.

Love come in many forms: it can be a loving relationship with our spouses and our children; love for our parents and our siblings; love for a dear friend; love for a stranger; love of the earth and its beauty. Have you ever given any thought about what love gives back to us? It actually brings us smiles, desires, caring, kindness, nurturing, happiness, contentment, knowledge, and a joy opening our hearts to a self-satisfaction and internal peace. All of these attribute to making our lives worthwhile, gives us a will and drive to do different things, a desire to live life to the fullest, a joy to exist on a daily basis, knowing we're doing our best with our lives.

Love lives in us and it familiarises us to enjoy existing upon this earth. Love and care is definitely not something you can buy, it's something acquired by who we're inside. It's a blessing to have the ability to love and care for others for who they are and not for what they are or what they have in life.

Without love and caring we would be lost in this country and in this world of ours. If there wasn't any love in our lives, we would go on aimlessly without purpose. Love and caring is a special gift given to us from God and we should use it as such.

The following inspirational story was told to me by my Nana Scully and it should remind us to take the time to tell the people we love and care about what we wish for them. The words of wisdom in this message are one that we can all share with those that are important to us in our lives.

'Recently I overheard a father and daughter in their last moments together at Galway airport. They had announced the departure. Standing near the security gate, they hugged and the father said: 'I love you, and I wish you enough.' The daughter replied: 'Dad, our life together has been more than enough. Your love is all I ever needed. I wish you enough, too, Dad.' They kissed and the daughter left.

The father walked over to the window where I was seated. Standing there I could see he wanted and needed to cry. I tried not to intrude on his privacy, but he welcomed me in by asking, "Did you ever say good-bye to someone knowing it would be forever?"

"Yes, I have," I replied. "Forgive me for asking, but why is this forever good-bye?"

"I am old, and she lives so far away. I have challenges ahead and the reality is – the next trip back will be for my funeral," he said.

"When you were saying good-bye, I heard you say, 'I wish you enough.' May I ask what that means?'"

He began to smile.

"That's a wish that has been handed down from other generations. My parents used to say it to everyone." He paused a moment and looked up as if trying to remember it in detail, and he smiled even more. "When we said, 'I wish you enough'; we were wanting the other person to have a life filled with just enough good things to sustain them so that others too could have enough."

Then turning toward me, he shared the following as if he were reciting it from memory.

I wish you enough sun to keep your attitude bright.

I wish you enough rain to appreciate the sun more.

I wish you enough happiness to keep your spirit alive.

I wish you enough pain so that the smallest joys in life appear much bigger.

I wish you enough gain to satisfy your wanting.

I wish you enough loss to appreciate all that you possess.

I wish you enough 'Hellos' to get you through the final 'Goodbye.'

A MOMENT IN TIME

They say it takes a minute to find a special person, an hour to appreciate them, a day to love them; but then an entire life to forget them. Remember to tell your family and friends that you wish them 'enough.'

TIME OUT

THIRTY-FIVE

IMPORTANCE OF STAYING POSITIVE

Staying positive is something that is available to everyone but taken up by far too few. Being positive doesn't imply that everything in your life is going well. We have all had times when we felt good, confident and on top of things. It is easy to stay positive during these times, but how do you tap into that positivity when life doesn't go as planned?

Most people can endure short periods of frustration, especially when there is a defined end in sight. The toughest times are when we look ahead and, for whatever reason, we feel that our situation is unending. We doubt our ability to endure our current condition for the long run. It is when you are in a situation that feels unbearable with no relief in sight that the future seems hopeless.

People who have survived such times are a source of great inspiration. Viktor Frankl in his book 'Man's Search for Meaning' describes the powerful psychological journey during his years in a concentration camp during World War Two. He tells us how he found the potential meaning of life even in conditions where he lost his family; he was stripped of all worldly belongings and lived day after day in miserable physical conditions. He fought back hopelessness and endured conditions beyond most people's imagination. He came to know first hand that while others can control your external existence, they cannot control your mind and he clung to his faith and beliefs that he would make it, and he did.

It takes courage to remain positive against negative forces. You have to remain true to yourself and your beliefs as to what is best for you even when you feel alone on this path. Anchor yourself with your own confidence and know that you can, and will, survive the challenges around you. Choose to have a positive outlook, bring those positive blessings to you by believing that it will come.

Imagine the best outcome in detail. Never give up. Keep believing and working towards your goals. Take care of yourself physically. Get enough sleep, eat a balanced diet and if you are physically capable, exercise a few times a week.

In today's world there is still hope for a happier future. If it's out of your hands, don't worry yourself. Ask yourself if worrying about it will make it better. Focus on the good things in your life. Make a list of the good things in your life. Be thankful for the good things in your life. Not all bad things are bad. Smile. It really does increase your face value

Gossip is an anchor that will weigh you down faster than anything else. Try to generate positive comments when you speak. Remember positive thinking begins with you. You have the power to spread smiles and encouraging thoughts. As soon as you open your mouth to speak, you are in charge of what comes out. Don't allow yourself to be a victim of the world around you. Smiles are free and contagious. If you want to spread something, try smiling. You will see how the world can become a happier place.

Use some positive thinking routines that will help you – when you are in a tough situation, imagine how it could be worse. Being an overseas development worker in some of the toughest places in the world, I have a job that makes this easy for me. I see people on my trips abroad that would love to have my problems compared to their own.

It can always be worse. I try to be a spiritual person and I find peace in letting go and believing that if I live with an open heart and help others and do the right thing that blessings will come my way and I will have what I need to be happy.

I have a personal faith that we are never burdened with more than we can handle. Bad things happen to good people. Crises happen that we can't understand. In my life I have witnessed unbelievable tragedies that caused me to ask every question there is about the meaning of life and the reason for suffering and pain.

This is a personal journey made by everyone, but in making this journey – realising that when everything outside of ourselves appears to be out of our control, we always have control of our own thinking.

A MOMENT IN TIME

Choose to be positive as much as you can and you will enrich your life and your journey through life and those around you who you love and care for.

TIME OUT

THIRTY-SIX

WHEN A FRIEND WALKS IN...

Good friends enrich our lives. Through a magical combination of similarities and differences, friends offer us the opportunity to know ourselves as we are and help us grow into who we want to be. Our similarities attract us to each other, comforting us with familiarity when we see ourselves in them. By acting as mirrors, friends help us define who we are by reflecting ourselves back to us.

Friends also help us know ourselves through our differences. Differences allow us to see other options and make choices about who we want to be. Sometimes we are drawn to those who appear to be our opposites, and we learn to accept the parts of them we love and the parts of them that don't resonate with us, allowing us a valuable learning experience.

Part of the joy of friendship is the feeling that we are accepted just the way we are, with no need to change. It is a gift they give us, and one we can give back.

Ultimately, we choose friends because they make us feel good about ourselves. Through tears and difficulties, friends help us find the laughter. When we find those special people who offer us that perfect combination of comfort and stimulus to grow, we are very fortunate.

To be a friend means that you are willing to give of yourself not only through the good times, but also during the bad times. There is an old Ethiopian proverb that says this so well: "A wise man remembers his friends at all times; a fool, only when he has need of them."

To be a friend means to encourage strengths in others wile

accepting their weaknesses; in other words, accepting them for who they are. A true friend is somebody who can make us do what we can. In the end, to be a true friend means giving freely and not expecting anything in return. A true friend feels your fears but fortifies your faith; sees your anxieties but frees your spirit; recognises your disabilities but emphasises your possibilities.

A MOMENT IN TIME

Always remember that a friend is someone who walks in when the whole world has walked away. Donal Rabbette was that friend in my life. May you always rest in peace and thanks for still looking after me.

THIRTY-SEVEN

A HEALTHY DOSE OF HUMILITY

Unfortunately in modern times we've developed some false connotations for the word 'humility' such as blind obedience, self-abasement, shyness, not standing up for ourselves or taking credit for our success.

In a highly individualised, competitive world where we must promote ourselves constantly to get jobs, be popular and succeed in many areas, the old fashioned notion of humility seems to only hold us back. However, the secret of 'humility' is that the more successful, the more recognised and loved you are, the harder it is to maintain and when we meet an admirable person with this virtue, it is beautiful beyond measure. 'Humility' is not putting yourself down or lacking pride, it is not excessive modesty or submissiveness. Rather, we achieve 'humility' when we completely conquer the Ego and when we do not see ourselves as superior to any other human being and when we are fully grateful for everything we have achieved and those who have helped us along the way. It's when we stop pushing others down so that we might step up and instead support each other arm in arm. It's not at all an easy state to achieve.

To be humble we must acknowledge that we are wrong sometimes. Accept feedback from others with grace and gratefulness, trying our best to learn from our mistakes rather than ignoring any suggestions that we don't want to hear. We must also take full responsibility for our failures and the consequences of these and not turn the blame on others. A large part of 'humility' is forgiveness. When we learn to forgive those who have wronged us and also to apologise to those we have wronged we step off our soapbox and learn that it is not our role to judge others. We must also endure unfair treatment with patience and grace, knowing that the world is not always fair but we can do our best to be so.

A humble person can be happy for others; can rejoice in their successes and achievements without feeling that they are any less because of them. With this we must try to only think and speak good things about others, celebrating their strengths rather than complaining about their flaws.

Gratefulness is another key element to humility. To not merely be successful and happy and beautiful, but grateful for every blessing we are given and every reward we work for. Also to be thankful to everyone who helps us along the way, no matter how small or great their aid may be, even having those that support and believe in you is immensely fortunate.

Give credit where it is due and show gratitude. A humble person is never above helping others. In fact they should look for opportunities to be of service and assistance to friends, family and strangers. However, to do so humbly is to not shout it from the rooftops, but rather do good deeds without any recognition or reward, to even remain anonymous in this charity. Perhaps the truest measure of 'humility' is in the way we treat others, with respect, kindness and compassion regardless of their age, gender, race or social status.

A humble person is kindest to those who have nothing to offer in return and will listen with as much attention to a child as to a king. These are not easy things to achieve, they are high goals to try to reach for and the true humble person fails to get there sometimes. Of all the beautiful people I have met though, those that are humble in their greatness are by far the most admirable. It takes a pure heart to soar high and still keep one's feet on the ground.

❀ ❀ ❀

Don't undermine your worth by comparing yourself to others,
It is because we are different that each of us is special. Don't set
your goals by what other people deem important. Only you
know what is best for you. Don't take for granted the things closest
to your heart. Cling to that as you would your life, for without
them life is meaningless. Don't let your life slip through your
fingers by living in the past or the future. By living your life one
day at a time, you live all the days of your life.

Don't give up when you still have something to give. Nothing
is really over ... until the moment you stop trying. Don't be afraid
to admit that you are less than perfect. It is the fragile thread that
binds us to each other. Don't be afraid to encounter risks. It's by
taking chances that we learn how to be brave. Don't shut love out
of your life by saying it's impossible to find. The quickest way to
receive love is to give love. The fastest way to lose love is to hold
on too tightly. And the best way to keep love is to give it wings.
Don't dismiss your dreams. To be without dreams is to be without
hope. To be without hope is to be without purpose. Don't run
through life so fast that you forget where you've been. But also
know where you're going. Life is not a race but a journey to be
savoured every step of the way. Live each day to the fullest.

A MOMENT IN TIME
*By keeping a healthy dose of humility in you lives, you are
constantly keeping yourself in check. Humility can be one of
the best psychological tools we humans have – the ability to
know that we aren't perfect, we aren't broken, we are who we
are and we are all very special and don't ever forget that.*

TIME OUT

THIRTY-EIGHT

HEAVEN CAN LEND A HELPING HAND

When we allow ourselves to understand the impact our actions have on ourselves, we realise the necessity to take loving action. We each have the power to correct conditions within as well as to affect the world we live in. There are so many ways to apply love in our everyday lives.

Yet, if we do not take care of ourselves and one another, it is virtually impossible to feel and share love with the world around us. As an act of self-love, we can begin to educate ourselves and learn to take care of our physical bodies as well as keep our thoughts and feelings positive and loving. Nurturing ourselves also teaches us how to nurture life around us and lend each other a helping hand.

Practise constant acts of kindness and you bring kindness upon yourself. Forgiveness is the easiest and most powerful act of kindness you can make. Both for you and for others, this activity promotes unity and harmony. Our lives are filled with opportunities to experience love, tolerance, peace and joy. When we, as individuals, realise our potential to love unconditionally, we transform ourselves and one another and the world we live in at the same time.

The choice is ours to create a world of joy and happiness, love and goodwill. Every moment of every day is a new beginning. The meaning held in these words opens us to a new way of living and experiencing life.

Start each day and each week as a new journey of self-discovery. Let go of yesterday and tomorrow and embrace the power of now. Remind yourself daily of the newness of life in the moment and learn to lend each other a helping hand. An old Irish fable might help to explain what I mean.

Paddy died and passed onto the next life. When he appeared before God, he passed all the questions and was allowed to enter heaven. He thanked God, but before he left for Heaven he made one request – a rather curious one at that. "May I visit Hell to see what it looks like"? The request was granted and Paddy stood at the fiery gates of Hell. The sights and the sounds stirred him to his depths. There was the weeping and wailing that he heard about. But there was something else that he had not heard about. Food lay all over the place in abundance. Despite the evident great supply of food everybody was suffering the agonies of starvation. Paddy was puzzled. Each person held a knife and a fork in their hands. There was plenty of food, so why the starvation? As he observed the plight, Paddy noticed that each one was able to pick up the food with their knives and forks, but were unable to get the food into their mouths because the knives and forks were to long. And the one unalterable rule of Hell was that each person must hold the knives and forks at the very end. This was Hell. Each one was completely centred on his or her own needs, unable to get satisfaction.

Then it was time for Paddy to go to heaven and when he got there, there was the joy and glory and happiness that he had heard about. But like hell there was something in heaven that he had also not heard about. Here he found a strange similarity to the conditions that prevailed in hell. There was the same pair of unusually long knives and forks. The exact unalterable rule was in effect, that each one must hold the knife and fork at the very end which again made it impossible for each person to reach their own mouth. But there was one big difference.

Each person was feeding their neighbour and each in turn was being fed by their neighbour. This was definitely Heaven. Each person was completely concerned about the needs of others. In this concern for their neighbour, their own needs were completely satisfied.

A MOMENT IN TIME

Take a look at the following poem

Heaven is really about being able to lend a helping hand:-

Beautiful hands are those that weave, bright threads of joy in lives that grieve.

Beautiful feet are those that run, on errands of mercy from sun to sun.

Beautiful lips are those that speak to comfort the mourner and hearten the weak;

Beautiful eyes are those that glow with the light of a spirit pure as snow.

Beautiful faces are those that seem with the very love of God to beam.

Beautiful forms are those that grace with gentle service the lowliest place.

Beautiful lives are those that bear for other lives their burden of care.

Beautiful souls are those that show The Spirit of God where're they go.

TIME OUT

THIRTY-NINE

DOING SOMETHING FOR OTHERS

Ever notice how you feel after doing something good for another person? When we perform a selfless act without any expectation, it can be so satisfying. Often after we make a difference in the life of another, we ask ourselves why we haven't done it more often.

Our act of selfless service might involve a kind word or lending an ear to a person who could use it. It could be holding the door open for a person we don't know. Or even as simple as smiling at someone we meet. We can help in many ways. When somebody is in need and we're open, there comes an impulse from inside us. It's at that instant in time, when we can choose to act upon it, or not. That moment tends to go by in a flash. Thoughts of a busy day ahead, or perhaps uncertainty, sometimes might sneak in and cloud our decision to move forward. And then it's passed.

The good news is that we can overcome our indecision by having already thought about selfless service and making it something that we do on an ongoing basis. Selfless acts performed consciously with thought-out intention magnify our satisfaction. We get that feeling of being truly alive and in the moment.

Consciously helping others is easy to do. We start by thinking of the reason why we would like to be of service. For example: "I'm going to help this person pick up those books they dropped." By doing this I am affirming that there are nice people in the world and that we're all looking out for each other. The action then follows and this becomes our truth.

At the end of the day, it's quite refreshing and healthy to feel good about ourselves. It's also very powerful to affect change by positively influencing the lives of those we touch. Even better, our selfless service to others has a way of attracting the same back to us. And when those acts of kindness happen to us, we feel right at home receiving them. The reason is because this has already become our model of how the world works. Everyday in your life can be then turned into a special occasion with no regrets.

A friend of mine opened his wife's clothes drawer and picked up a silk paper wrapped package: "This," he said "isn't any ordinary package." He unwrapped the box and stared at both the silk paper and the box. "She got this the first time we went to New York , eight or nine years ago. She has never put it on. Was saving it for a special occasion. Well, I guess this is it."

He got near the bed and placed the gift box next to the other clothing he was taking to the funeral house, his wife had just died. He turned to me and said: "Never save something for a special occasion. Every day in your life is a special occasion."

I think those words changed my life. Now I read more and clean less. I sit on the beach in Salthill at times without worrying about anything. I have started to spend more time with my family and less at work. I understood that life should be a source of experience to be lived up to – not survived through. I no longer keep anything.

The words "Someday..." and "One Day..." are fading away from my dictionary. If it's worth seeing, listening or doing, I want to see, listen or do it now. I don't know what my friend's wife would have done if she knew she wouldn't be there the next morning, this nobody can tell.

I think she might have called her relatives and closest friends.

She might call old friends to make peace over past quarrels. I'd like to think she would go out for her favourite food. It's these small things that I would regret not doing, if I knew my time had come. I would regret it, because I'd no longer see the friends I would meet, and the letters or e-mails...that I wanted to write "one of these days".

I would regret and feel sad, because I didn't say to my parents, my brother and sisters, wife and daughters, not enough times at least, how much I love them. Now, I try not to delay, postpone or keep anything that could bring laughter and joy into our lives. And, on each morning, I say to myself that this could be a special day to do a selfless act for others. Each day, each hour, each minute, is special.

A MOMENT IN TIME

Keep in mind how special each day and each week can be if we consciously set about helping those in need and do some selfless service with our lives. Everyday of your life is and should be a special occasion. Only you can make it so.

TIME OUT

FORTY

LOVE DOESN'T NEED A REASON

I worked for many years with the charity GOAL and now work for Self Help Africa. I suppose you could say that the developing world and Africa are in my blood. Sure aren't my two daughters Mia and Sophie from Ethiopia. Well a number of years ago while working in Angola I buried a street child, called Cantora at the age of 15. Cantora and I knew one another for about three years and I believe that God brought him into my life. He was a street child who attended one of our nightly feeding stations on the streets of Luanda, the capital city of Angola.

Cantora and many of the other 2,000 street children that we fed at night at feeding stations around the city taught me to love life. Cantora taught me to be thankful for life even though, at times, it is hard to do so. Life for Cantora was never easy but he never gave up on God or life. He always found the faith to believe and the will and tenacity to live amidst the challenges of his life – be it homelessness, addiction, prison and even AIDS from which he eventually died.

Shortly before he died, he made a passing lament that he did not have anyone to love him. I told him, "Cantora, for whatever it's worth: I fed you each night through the help of GOAL for three years and I want to say 'I love you.'"

He started crying. It is indeed surprising that Cantora and many of the street children in Angola and I clicked so well because we are just so different; we are poles apart in terms of life experience or background or race or even language. I suspect that were it not for God who brought us together in those three years, Cantora and I probably would never have met. Yet, despite our differences, God blessed me with the life of this child and many street children on the streets of Angola. And I hope that somehow, in my imperfect and bumbling ways, I have made some difference in the life of Cantora and many of the street children I cared for in my work with GOAL. But what if I did not open my heart to make room for these street and abandoned children in my life, children who were totally different from me and from the life I had grown up in as a child? Then it would have been tragic...tragic that I would miss one of God's blessings. God's blessings come in gift packages that are perhaps not often attractive to us.

We have somehow learned that there must be a reason to love someone. So we set up criteria by which we judge those we must love, and those we should exclude from our love. We have learned that there are some who are worthy of love, while others we can ignore. We have learned to love only those who are like us and at the same time, we've learned to close our lives from those who are different from us or not likable for whatever reason. But what if, for the moment, we lay aside our prejudices and open our hearts to those we would like to dismiss? Then perhaps, we might just find them to be God's blessings. God has given each one of us a heart to love.

It is through our hearts by which he comes to show love and compassion to the world. As God is generous beyond our imaginings, this gift of love is something we must extend not just to a worthy few but to everyone, regardless of our natural inclination or prejudices and reasonings to reject or exclude. We must extend hospitality, compassion and love to those who are easy for us to ignore or dismiss. For love simply is. Love doesn't need a reason, love doesn't always rhyme. But what we got is a heart to love. Simply use it. Simply give love away.

We must welcome everyone without discrimination. Despite our past mistakes, despite our present injustices towards one another, we must welcome each other with love and forgiveness. God turns no one away. This kind of love and hospitality is beyond our comprehension. Why would God squander his love on us? God's love needs no reason; God's love doesn't always rhyme with human reason. God simply is beyond human comprehension. Likewise, it is the same radical hospitality we must extend to everyone, without prejudice, without discrimination. For love doesn't need a reason.

A MOMENT IN TIME

May God bless you with tears to shed for those who suffer from pain, rejection, starvation and war. So that you may reach out your hand to comfort them and turn their pain into joy. And may God bless you with enough foolishness to believe that you can make a difference in this world. So that you can do what others claim cannot be done.

TIME OUT

FORTY-ONE

HAVE A CHILD'S MINDSET

When you think about toddlers, or are blessed to experience them yourself, like myself and my wife Jacqui have been recently, you come to a realisation that they are always on the move, never wanting to stop. They go through each day with so much enthusiasm and never seem to tire. They coast through their early years often with no real trouble and usually with a smile on their faces.

Children have something about them that we've lost somewhere along the way. They have the ability to forgive quickly, not really worry and get frustrated over things. They just enjoy the simple things in life. They don't hold grudges or resentments against anyone and if for some strange reason they do, it is usually only temporary as normally they will be playing and interacting with them the next day on the playground.

I had experiences with my two daughters Mia and Sophie recently when I walked in their room and they were in their bed and cot. They jumped up and down, screaming with happiness and great big smiles on their faces. I wondered what they were smiling and happy about. Was it their birthday? Was it Christmas? Were we leaving on holidays to Offaly or Clare?

The answer to those questions is no... they were just excited about a new day and could not wait to start it. That is where I thought to myself... Why can't adults be like this? When did we lose our buzz for life? How can we get it back and keep it?

Too many times as adults, we forget how to live happily and

the days seem to slip by. Sometimes people tend to mope around over a variety of things that are out of their control like the weather or something that happened to them in the past, or even something as silly as someone talking about them at the coffee shop or local pub.

In too many instances people live not just one day like this, but many. They can't get that day or other days back... ever. They repeatedly sob and sulk and in the interim, try to bring others to their level.

We are not on this earth to be miserable. We are on it to take each day and make the best out of it. To face new challenges and grow from them. To share our joy and happiness in the event that someone else will be positively affected by it.

Our emotions are contagious to people that surround us, be it strangers or loved ones. We need to take a lesson from our children and seize the day. We are not on this earth for infinity, but only for a short time.

A MOMENT IN TIME

Go back to when you were a child and live without the troublesome melancholy that can seem to swallow you up at times. Make your whole day a game of sorts, and when tomorrow comes, play it again but this time, do it better.

FORTY-TWO

NEW YEAR CODE OF ETHICS

Rise with the sun to pray. Pray alone. Pray often. God will listen, if you only speak. Be tolerant of those who are lost on their path. Ignorance, conceit, anger, jealousy and greed stem from a lost soul. Pray that they will find guidance. Search for yourself, be yourself. Do not allow others to make your path for you. It is your road and yours alone. Others may walk it with you but no one can walk it for you. Treat the guests in your home with much consideration. Serve them the best food, give them the best beds and treat them with respect and honour.

Do not take what is not yours whether from a person, a community, the wilderness or from a culture. If it was not earned or given, it's not yours. Respect all things that are placed upon this earth – whether it's person, animal or plant. Honour other people's thoughts, wishes and words. Never interrupt another or mock or rudely mimic them. Allow each person the right to personal expression. Never speak of others in a bad way. The negative energy that you put out into the world will multiply when it returns to you. All persons make mistakes. And all mistakes can be forgiven. Bad thoughts cause illness of the mind, body and spirit. Practise optimism.

Nature is not for us, it is a part of us. They are part of your worldly family. Children are the seeds of our future. Plant love in their hearts and water them with wisdom and life's lessons. When they are grown, give them space to grow. Avoid hurting the hearts of others especially those of children. The poison of your pain will return to you. Be truthful at all times. Honesty is the test of ones will within this world. Keep yourself balanced. Your mental self, spiritual self, emotional self, and physical self

– all need to be strong, pure and healthy. Work out the body to strengthen the mind. Grow rich in spirit to cure emotional ailments.

Make conscious decisions as to who you will be and how you will react. Be responsible for your own actions. Respect the privacy and personal space of others. Do not touch the personal property of others. Be true to yourself first. You cannot nurture and help others if you cannot nurture and help yourself first. Respect others beliefs. Do not force your belief on others. Share your good fortune with others. Participate in charity.

The following poem called 'One' I came across on a wall in one of Mother Teresa houses for the physically unwell goes as follows: 'One song can spark a moment; one flower can wake the dream. one tree can start a forest, one bird can herald spring. One smile begins a friendship, one handclasp lifts a soul. One star can guide a ship at sea, one word can frame the goal. One vote can change a nation, one sunbeam lights a room. One candle wipes out darkness, one laugh will conquer gloom. One step must start each journey; one word must start each prayer. One hope will raise our spirits; one touch can show you care. One voice can speak with wisdom. One heart can know what's true. One life can make the difference; you see it's up to you.'

A MOMENT IN TIME

Never forget how very important and how very special each and every one of us is in this life.

FORTY-THREE

LEARNING ABOUT TEAMWORK AND LEADERSHIP

I had the good fortune to be on RTE's Operation Transformation programme a few years ago. It is predominately about leadership and teamwork. Dr. Eddie, who is one of the experts, told me to look up the story about the Tortoise and the Hare. Although I already knew that story off by heart I re-read it as directed.

Once upon a time a hare and a tortoise had an argument about who was the faster. They decided to settle the argument with a race. They agreed on a route and started off the race. The hare shot ahead and ran quickly for some time. Then seeing that he was far ahead of the tortoise, he thought he'd sit under a tree for some time and relax before continuing the race. He sat under the tree and fell asleep. The tortoise, plodding on, overtook him and finished the race as the undisputed champ. The hare woke up and realised that he'd lost the race. The moral of the story is that slow and steady wins the race. This is the version of the story that we've all grown up with.

But the older version of the story which I didn't know before then was a more interesting version of this story. The hare was disappointed at losing the race and he did some soul-searching. He realised that he'd lost the race because he had been overconfident. If he had not taken things for granted, there's no way the tortoise could have won. So he challenged the tortoise to another race. The tortoise agreed. This time, the hare went all out and ran without stopping from start to finish. He won easily. The moral of the story? Fast and consistent will always beat the slow and steady.

The tortoise did some thinking this time and realised that there's no way he could beat the hare in a race the way it was currently set out. He thought for a while and then challenged the hare to another race but on a slightly different route. The hare agreed. They started off. In keeping with his self-made commitment to be consistently fast, the hare took off and ran at top speed until he came to a broad river. The finishing line was a couple of miles on the other side of the river.

The hare sat there wondering what to do. In the meantime the tortoise trundled along, got into the river, swam to the opposite bank, continued walking and finished the race.

The moral of the story? First identify your core competency and then change the playing field to suit that competency.

The hare and the tortoise, by this time, had become pretty good friends and they did some thinking together. Both realised that the last race could have been run much better. So they decided to do the last race again, but to run as a team this time. They started off and this time, the hare carried the tortoise to the riverbank. There, the tortoise took over and swam across with the hare on his back. On the opposite bank, the hare again carried the tortoise and they reached the finishing line together. They both felt a greater sense of satisfaction than they'd felt earlier.

The moral of the story now?

It's good to be individually brilliant and to have strong core competencies but unless you're able to work in a team and harness each other's core competencies, you'll always perform below par because there will always be situations at which you'll do poorly and someone else does well.

Teamwork is mainly about situational leadership, letting the person with the relevant core competency for a situation take leadership.

There are more lessons to be learned from this story. Note that neither the hare nor the tortoise gave up after failures. The hare decided to work harder and put in more effort after his failure. The tortoise changed his strategy because he was already working as hard as he could. In life, when faced with failure, sometimes it is appropriate to work harder and put in more effort. Sometimes it is appropriate to change strategy and try something different. And sometimes it is appropriate to do both. The hare and the tortoise also learned another vital lesson. When we stop competing against a rival and instead start competing against the situation, we perform far better.

A MOMENT IN TIME
We can learn a vital lesson from this story if we stop competing against a rival and instead start competing against the situation and you will find that you will perform far better.

TIME OUT

FORTY-FOUR

EACH DAY IS A GIFT

My wife's mother, Kay who is 79 years of age, is such a beautiful woman who is always well-poised and who is fully dressed each morning by 7 o'clock, with her hair sorted and make up perfectly applied even though she suffers terribly from arthritis. She has been quite unwell for a while and we got her a bed for treatment in one of the Galway hospitals.

After many hours of waiting patiently in the lobby area of the hospital, she smiled sweetly when told her room was ready. As she manoeuvred her walker to the elevator, I provided a visual description of her tiny room, including the eyelet curtains that had been hung on her window.

'I love it', she stated with the enthusiasm of an eight year old having just been presented with a new puppy. 'Mrs O'Grady, you haven't seen the room. Just wait,' I said.

'That doesn't have anything to do with it,' she replied. 'Happiness is something you decide on ahead of time. Whether I like the room or not doesn't depend on how the furniture is arranged, it's how I arrange my mind. I've already decided to love it. It's a decision I make every morning when I wake up. I have a choice, I can spend the day in bed recounting the difficulty I have with the parts of my body that no longer work, or get out of bed and be thankful for the ones that do.'

'Each day is a gift and, as long as my eyes are open, I'll focus on the new day and all the happy memories I've stored away, just for this time in my life.'

She went on to explain: 'Old age is like a bank account, you withdraw from it what you've put in. So, my advice to Ronan is to deposit a lot of happiness in the bank account of memories and life. 'And, thank you for your part in filling my memory bank,' she added. 'I am still depositing'.

'Remember the five simple rules to being happy. First, free your heart from greed. Second, free your mind from worries. Third, live simply. Fourth, give more. And fifth, expect less,' she added.

As Rather Walker once wrote in her Beatitudes for friends of the aged: 'Blessed are they who understand my faltering step and palsied hand. Blessed are they who know that my ears today must strain to catch the things they say. Blessed are they who seem to know that my eyes are dim and my wits are slow. Blessed are they who looked away when coffee was spilled at the table today. Blessed are they with cheery smiles that stop to chat for a little while. Blessed are they who never say, 'You've told that story twice.'

Blessed are they who know the ways to bring back memories of yesterday. Blessed are they who make it known that I'm loved, respected and not alone. Blessed are they who know I'm at a loss to find strength to carry the cross. Blessed are they who ease the days on my journey home in loving ways and who make each day of my life a gift.'

Thank you Kay for helping to make each day of my life a gift. You are an example of how each of us can make more of our own lives and those of our families and friends in tough and austere times.

A MOMENT IN TIME

Remember that each day is a gift and many of our elderly and aged friends and relatives helped to provide us with such a gift.. Let's look after our elderly now and always.

TIME OUT

FORTY-FIVE

EVERYONE SHOULD BE ALLOWED TO PLAY

I was at a meeting recently to help organise the Maynooth to Galway charity cycle of which I was a founding member. The year before it made close on €86,000 for Pieta House – a fantastic charity supporting mental illness and suicide prevention. This year was our 25th year of the event and we chose Down Syndrome Ireland, a charity that is very close to my heart and in the end we raised over €150,000 for them.

I was thinking as I drove from Maynooth to Galway with my friend, Gary, how great it was to be able to help people and especially children in need in this present climate. When a Down Syndrome child comes into our world, an opportunity to realise true human nature presents itself. It comes in the way other people treat that child whether the child is unwell or has some other specific need. I suppose the following story from my Nana Scully's prayer book might help me explain what I am trying to say.

Darragh and his father had walked past a field where some boys he knew were playing football. Darragh asked: 'Do you think they'll let me play.'

His father knew that most of the boys would not want someone like Darragh on their team, but he also understood that if his son was allowed to play, it would give him a much needed sense of belonging and some confidence to be accepted by others in spite of his handicaps.

The father tentatively approached one of the boys and asked if Darragh could play. The boy looked around for guidance and said: 'We're losing by six points and the match is in the second-half. I guess he can be on our team and we'll try to put him in to the forwards in a while.'

Darragh struggled over to the team's dugout and put on a team jersey with such a broad smile that his father had a small tear in his eye as he watched. The boys too saw the father's joy. With 10 minutes to go, Darragh's team scored a few points but were still behind by three. In the next few minutes Darragh was put in at corner forward.

Even though no balls came his way, he was obviously ecstatic just to be in the game and on the field, grinning from ear to ear as his father waved to him from the sidelines. With five minutes to go, Darragh's team scored again.

Now, behind by just two points, the potential winning goal was a possibility and Darragh based himself just outside the large square. At this juncture, do they pass the ball to Darragh and give away their chance to win the game? Surprisingly, Darragh was given the ball. Everyone knew that a goal was all but impossible because Darragh didn't even know how to hold the ball properly, much less connect with the ball.

However, as Darragh stepped up to collect the ball, the defender, recognising that his team had put their thoughts of winning the game aside for this moment in Darragh's life, moved back a few steps to let Darragh gather the ball so that he could at least make contact and have a clear shot on the goal. Darragh swung his right foot and hit a slow ground ball straight past the 'keeper into the bottom corner of the net. Everyone yelled and screamed and he was cheered as the hero who scored the goal that won the game for his team.

That day the boys on both teams helped bring a piece of true love and humanity into this world. Darragh died that winter, having never forgotten the day he played the role of hero, making his father so happy and coming home and seeing his mother tearfully embrace her little man of the match.

A MOMENT IN TIME

Try to look at opportunities to realise true examples of how we can make life better for other human beings and especially children. We can and we should.

TIME OUT

FORTY-SIX

WELL TODAY I DIDN'T DO IT

"Help, I'm a working mom." It's a common cry and one many women understand. If you are a mom, you are a working mom. You don't have to collect a salary; all you have to have is someone who calls you "mom" and relies on you. Reality for many mothers is having too much to do and not enough time to do it.

I remember my mother trying to work outside the home, getting up early, getting children ready for school while trying to get herself ready for work. They say the first half hour sets the tone for the rest of the day. If so, my mother's tone was set at stress before she left the house. She then had to go to work and deal with the pressure of the workplace, try to perform her duties, while thinking about her children. At work, the home workday would just begin: helping us kids get homework started, getting dinner ready, washing the dishes, getting the laundry started, refereeing fights. In truth a mother's work is never done and sometimes we don't seem to notice what's involved. A funny story I heard from a friend recently might help to explain.

A man came home from work and found his three children outside, still in their pyjamas, playing in the mud, with empty food boxes and wrappers strewn around the garden. The door of his wife's car was open, as was the front door to the house and no sign of the dog. Walking in the door he found an even bigger mess. A lamp had been knocked over, the throw rug was against one wall. In the front room the TV was on loudly with the cartoon channel, the family room was strewn with toys and various items of clothing.

In the kitchen, dishes filled the sink, breakfast food was spilled on the counter, the fridge door was open wide, dog food was spilled on the floor, a broken glass lay under the table and a small pile of sand was spread by the back door.

He quickly headed up the stairs, stepping over toys and more piles of clothes, looking for his wife. He was worried she might be ill or that something serious had happened. He was met with a small trickle of water as it made its way out the bathroom door. As he peered inside he found wet towels, scummy soap and more toys strewn over the floor. Miles of toilet paper lay in a heap and toothpaste had been smeared over the mirror and walls. As he rushed to the bedroom, he found his wife still curled up in the bed in her pyjamas, reading a novel.

She looked up at him, smiled and asked how his day went. He looked at her bewildered and asked: 'What happened here today?'

She again smiled and answered: "You know every day when you come home from work and you ask me what in the world do I do all day?"

"Yes," was his incredulous reply.

She answered: "Well, today I didn't do it."

A MOMENT IN TIME
Try to empathise with those close to you and, at times of stress in their lives, try to see things from their point of view.

FORTY-SEVEN

RECOGNISE YOUR OWN UNIQUE SONG

Have you ever stopped to think what a brilliant, unique and remarkable person you are? Of all the people who ever lived, not one of them is just like you. No one who ever lived had the abilities, limits, talents, appearance, happiness, sorrows, opportunities, burdens, and possibilities that you have. No one has exactly the same thoughts as you do. No one speaks exactly as you do. No one prays just as you do. No one loves all the same people that love you. Even the ones, who laugh like you, don't sneeze like you. The ones, who cry like you, don't have the same sorrow you do. The ones, who smile like you, don't know the same joys that you do.

No one before and no one yet to come has your gifts. You weren't meant to be like anyone else. You don't need to change to show that you're different. You were meant to be special. At no time in all history will the same things be going on in someone else's mind, soul, and spirit, as with you this very moment. If you did not exist, there would be a gap in our lives, a change in our history, a hole in our creation, and something missing from God's plan. Cherish your uniqueness. It is a gift given only to you.

No one can speak your words. No one can cry your tears. No one can impart your cheer and joy. No one can smile your smile. No one can bring your unique impact to another human heart. No one can take your place. The gift of uniqueness was given to you to tell about and to enjoy. Let it inform and inspire you. Reach out to others with your life. Share yourself along life's pathway. You are God's gift and unique to this world. As usual a story might help to explain about what I mean about your uniqueness and it comes from a story I heard about life in a African tribe.

When a woman in a certain African tribe knows she is pregnant, she goes out into the wilderness with a few friends and together they pray and meditate until they hear the song of the child. They recognise that every soul has its own vibration that expresses its unique flavour and purpose. When the women attune to the song, they sing it out loud. Then they return to the tribe and teach it to everyone else. When the child is born, the community gathers and sings the child's song to him or her.

Later, when the child enters education, the village gathers and chants the child's song. When the child passes through the initiation to adulthood, the people again come together and sing. At the time of marriage, the person hears his or her song. Finally, when the soul is about to pass from this world, the family and friends gather at the person's bed, just as they did at their birth, and they sing the person to the next life.

In the African tribe there is one other occasion upon which the villagers sing to the child. If at any time during his or her life, the person commits a crime or aberrant social act, the individual is called to the centre of the village and the people in the community form a circle around them. Then they sing their song to them. The tribe recognises that the correction for anti-social behaviour is not punishment; it is love and the remembrance of identity.

When you recognise your own song, you have no desire or need to do anything that would hurt another. A friend is someone who knows your song and sings it to you when you have forgotten it. Those who love you are not fooled by mistakes you have made or dark images you hold about yourself. They remember your beauty when you feel ugly; your wholeness when you are broken; your innocence when you feel guilty; and your purpose when you are confused.

You may not have grown up in an African tribe that sings your song to you at crucial life transitions, but life is always reminding you when you are in tune with yourself and when you are not. When you feel good, what you are doing matches your song, and when you feel awful, it doesn't. In the end, we shall all recognise our song and sing it well. You may feel a little wobbly at the moment, but so have all the great singers. So remember, just keep singing and you'll find your way home.

A MOMENT IN TIME

Make a new start to your life this week and show that we can win the world by love and not by hatred.

TIME OUT

FORTY-EIGHT

WHEN A GESTURE
MEANS A LOT

The man slowly looked up. This was a woman clearly very wealthy. 'Leave me alone,' he growled. The woman continued standing. 'Are you hungry?' she asked.

'No,' he answered sarcastically. 'I've just come from dining with the President. Now go away.'

The woman smiled. Suddenly the man felt a hand under his arm. 'What are you doing?' the man asked. 'Leave me alone'.

Just then a garda came up. 'Is there a problem?' he asked.

'No,' the woman answered. 'I'm just trying to get this man to his feet. Will you help?'

The garda said: 'That's old Sean. He's been a fixture around here for a couple of years. What do you want with him?'

'See that cafe over there?' she asked. 'I'm going to get him something to eat.'

'Are you crazy?' Sean interjected. 'I don't want to go in there.' Then he felt strong hands grab his other arm and lift him up. 'This is a good deal, Sean,' the garda answered. 'Don't blow it.' Finally, they got Sean into the cafe. The manager strode across the cafe.

'What's going on here?' he asked. 'Is this man in trouble?'

'This lady brought this man in here to be fed,' the garda answered. 'Not in here,' the manager replied angrily. 'Having a person like that here is bad for business.'

Old Sean smiled. 'I told you so. Now let me go.' The woman turned to the manager. 'Sir, are you familiar with Scully and Associates, the Philanthropies Company?'

'Of course I am,' the manager answered. 'They hold their

weekly meetings here.'

'And do you make a large amount of money providing food for these meetings?'

'What business is that of yours?'

"I am the CEO of the company.'

'Oh,' the manager said.

'I thought that might make a difference.'

She asked the garda, who was busy stifling a giggle, 'Would you like to join us?"

'No thanks, I'm on duty.'

'Maybe a tea to go?'

'Yes, ma'am. That would be nice.'

The manager said, 'I'll get your tea right away.'

'You certainly put him in his place,' the garda said.

'That was not my intent. I have a reason for all this,' she explained.

She sat down with Sean. "Do you remember me?'

Sean said, 'I think so – you look familiar.'

'I'm a little older,' she said. 'I came through that very door, cold and hungry. I was just out of college,' the woman began. 'I had come to the midlands looking for a job but found nothing. Finally I was down to my last few pennies. I walked around for days. It was January and I was cold and nearly starving. I saw this place and walked in on the off chance that I could get something to eat.'

Sean lit up with a smile. 'Now I remember,' he said. 'I was serving. You came up and asked me if you could work for something to eat. I said that it was against company policy.'

'I know,' the woman continued. 'Then you made me the biggest sandwich that I had ever seen, gave me a cup of tea, and told me to enjoy it. I was afraid that you would get into trouble. Then, when I looked over, I saw you put the price of my food in the cash register. I knew then that everything would be all right.'

'So you started your own business?' old Sean said.

'I got a job that very day. I worked my way up. Eventually I started my own business that prospered.'

She gave Sean her business card. 'When you are finished here, I want you to pay a visit to a Mr. Lyons. He's my personnel director. I'll go talk to him now and I'm certain he'll find something for you to do.'

She smiled. 'I think he might even find the funds to give you a little advance so that you can buy some clothes and get a place to live. If you ever need anything, my door is always open.'

There were tears in the old man's eyes. 'How can I ever thank you?' he said. 'Don't thank me,' the woman answered. 'To God goes the glory. He led me to you.'

Outside the cafe, the garda and the woman paused at the entrance before going their separate ways. 'Thank you for all your help,' she said. 'On the contrary,' he answered. 'Thank you. I saw a miracle today, something that I will never forget. And thank you for the tea.'

A MOMENT IN TIME

Never underestimate the power of your actions. With one small gesture you can change a person's life and remember what goes around, comes around.

TIME OUT

FORTY-NINE

MAKE A DIFFERENCE IN SOMEONE'S LIFE

Life at the moment in our country is very tough but if we can strive to share a bit of kindness every day, and care for those who suffer pain and strife and if we try to understand, we can make a difference in someone's life.

There is no better thing that you can do in life than to help someone, care for someone or love someone. If we try to concentrate on all the positive moments that touch our everyday lives instead of all the negativity that is going around, we will radiate a positivism of life to those around us and open the window of optimism for a new tomorrow. Everybody has something to offer. Indeed, most of us have many things to offer and in a lot of cases, special expertise is not required. We are all capable of giving that which people need most of all: Love. Love translates into time, service and the sharing of oneself. An old anonymous story might help in making us see how each one of us if we try can make a difference.

A teacher in a school decided to honour her Leaving Cert students by telling them the difference they each made. First she told them how the student made a difference to her and the class. Then she presented each of them with a blue ribbon imprinted on it: "Who I Am Makes a Difference."

Afterwards the teacher decided to do a class project to see what kind of impact 'recognition' would have on a community. She gave each of the students three more ribbons and instructed them to go out and spread this acknowledgment ceremony.

One of the boys in the class went to a junior executive in a nearby company and honoured him for helping him with his career planning. He gave him a blue ribbon. Then he gave him two extra ribbons, and said: "We're doing a class project on recognition, and we'd like you to go out, find somebody to honour, give them a blue ribbon, then give them the extra blue ribbon so they can acknowledge a third person to keep this acknowledgment ceremony going."

Later that day the junior executive went in to see his boss, who had been noted as being kind of a grouchy fellow. He told his boss that he deeply admired him for being a creative genius. The boss seemed very surprised. The junior executive asked him if he would accept the gift of the blue ribbon. His surprised boss said, "Well, sure." The junior executive placed the blue ribbon on his boss's jacket. As he gave him the last extra ribbon, he said: "Would you take this extra ribbon and pass it on by honouring somebody else? The young boy who first gave me the ribbons is doing a project in school and we want to keep this recognition ceremony going and find out how it affects people."

That night the boss came home to his young daughter and sat her down. He said: "The most incredible thing happened to me today. I was in my office and one of the junior executives came in and told me he admired me and gave me a blue ribbon for being a creative genius. Imagine. He thinks I'm a creative genius."

Then he put this blue ribbon that says "Who I Am Makes a Difference" on my jacket. He gave me an extra ribbon and asked me to find somebody else to honour. As I was driving home tonight, I started thinking about who I would honour with this ribbon and I thought about you. "My days are really hectic and when I come home I don't pay a lot of attention to you. Sometimes

I scream at you for not getting good enough grades in school and for your bedroom being a mess, but somehow tonight, I just wanted to sit here and, well, just let you know that you do make a difference to me. Aside from your mother, you are the most important person in my life. You're a great child and I love you."

The startled girl couldn't stop crying. Her whole body shook. She looked up at her father and said through her tears: "I was planning on doing something really bad to myself tomorrow, Dad, because I didn't think you loved me. Now I don't need to because I know you truly do."

Don't lose sight of what's important. Don't lose hope when life gets tough. Don't give up on your dreams for the future. Don't sell yourself short in life. Don't forget how to laugh. Don't be too proud to cry. Don't be hateful or hurtful. Don't forget to say, "thank you" and "I love you" each and every day. Don't expect there will always be a tomorrow. Don't forget to smell the roses. Don't forget that one small kindness pays you back two fold.

A MOMENT IN TIME

Please don't forget that each and every one of us is special in our own unique and individual way. Most of all remember that each day God's love shines down upon us and gives us an insight into how loving and caring for others can make such a tremendous difference.

TIME OUT

FIFTY

OUR BLESSINGS CAN BE MERCIES IN DISGUISE

A prayer takes just a matter of seconds to utter, but its influence on our lives can be permanent. A simple prayer can change us; can lead us on the path to healing ourselves and our world.

Pray for peace, pray for healing, pray for love, pray for advances in science, like the award for cancer research that was awarded to some of the staff in NUIG a while ago, pray for the strength to eradicate poverty and disease, pray to overcome injustice, pray for resolve, pray for others, pray for yourself.

Pray to God with all your heart and soul and then gather up your might to meet the challenges that lie ahead. In the current climate we need help and strength to make the lives of our children brighter, so let's get doing it for our beautiful children.

Prayer is not a passive activity. Prayer awakens us. Our eyes begin to notice beauty where we never noticed it before. Our hearts begin to feel compassion we never knew we had. Our priorities shift. As we talk to God, we receive the encouragement to live up to the potential inside us. Soon we start to see beyond ourselves into the world that is waiting for our help.

God's answer to our prayers may be very different from the answer we were searching for. God's reply might come as the strength to fight on. It may come as the courage to face what we have feared. It may be the ability to accept what we have been denying. Or it may appear as hope in the face of despair. We are not alone. God is present in our lives. When we stop bargaining with God and start opening up, our prayers suddenly start working. We can pray for strength and receive strength. Prayer is ultimately an experience, not a request. It is a sense of being connected, of being part of something larger than ourselves. It is an attempt to be in the presence of God.

One of my favourite songs in life is by Laura Story which explains that sometimes our blessings are mercies in disguise.

A MOMENT IN TIME

May you feel the loving presence of those who hold you in their thoughts and prayers. May your spirit find what it needs to sustain you on this journey of life. May you discover your inner strength and face all difficulties with dignity and grace.

FIFTY-ONE

NUDGE THE BALANCE

In life it is faith that starts us off but it is charity that keeps us going in any undertaking. Little acts of charity can awaken life-giving confidence in us all. Charity can be enacted in many ways, such as giving food and clothes to the needy, cheerful care of the sick, a warm greeting or smile to the people that you meet, or even listening to a friend's worries. As the saying goes 'Charity sees the need not the cause'. I heard a great story in Nepal which might help to explain what I am saying.

'A 91-year-old woman died after living a very long dignified life. When she met God, she asked Him something that had really bothered her for a very long time. "If man was created in God's image, and if all people are created equal, why do people treat each other so badly?"

God replied that each person has a unique lesson to teach us. It is only through these lessons that we learn about life, people and our relationships with God. This confused the woman, so God began to explain:

"When someone lies to you, it teaches you that things are not always what they seem. The truth is often beneath the surface. Look beyond the masks people wear if you want to know what is in their hearts. When someone steals from you, it teaches you that nothing is forever. Always appreciate what you have. You never know when you might lose it. Never take your friends or family for granted. When someone inflicts injury upon you, it teaches you that the human state is a very fragile one.

Protect and take care of your body as best as you can; it's the one thing that you are sure to have forever. When someone mocks you, it teaches you that no two people are alike. When you encounter people who are different from you, do not judge them by how they look or act. Instead, base it on the contents of what is in their hearts.

When someone breaks your heart, it teaches you that loving someone does not always mean that the person will love you back. But don't turn your back on love because when you find the right person, the joy that one person brings you will make up for all of your past hurts. When someone holds a grudge against you, it teaches you that everyone makes mistakes.

When you are wronged, the most virtuous thing you can do is forgive the offender without pretence. Forgiving those who have hurt us is often the most difficult and painful of life's experiences, but it is also the most courageous thing a person can do. When a loved one is unfaithful to you, it teaches you that resisting temptation is man's greatest challenge. Be vigilant in your resistance against all temptations. By doing so, you will be rewarded with an enduring sense of satisfaction far greater than the temporary pleasure by which you were tempted. Aspire to make your dreams come true. Do not feel guilty about your success but never let an obsession with achieving your goals lead you to engage in malevolent activities. When someone ridicules you, it teaches you that nobody is perfect. Accept people for their merits and be tolerant of their flaws.'

Upon hearing the Lord's wisdom, the old woman became concerned that there are no lessons to be learned from people's good deeds and works of charity. God replied that Man's capacity to love is the greatest gift He has. Each act of love also teaches us a lesson. The woman's curiosity deepened. God, once again began to explain: "When someone loves us, it teaches us love, kindness, charity, honesty, humility, forgiveness, acceptance, and all of these can counteract all the evil in the world. For every good deed, there is one evil deed. Man alone has the power to control the balance between good and evil, but because the lessons of love are not taught often enough, the power is too often abused.

When you enter someone's life, whether by plan, chance or coincidence, consider what your lesson will be. Will you teach love or a harsh lesson of reality? When you die, will your life have resulted in more loving or more hurting? More comfort or more pain? More joy or more sadness? Each one of us has the power over the balance of the love in the world. Use it wisely."

A MOMENT IN TIME
Grab the opportunity to nudge the world's scale of love in the right direction.

TIME OUT

FIFTY-TWO

NO ONE MAKES IT ALONE

Nowadays, it is fashionable to think of yourself first. In relationships, we are urged to make others happy by making ourselves happy. Our careers, our interests and our personal ambitions are a priority. With self-centredness the norm, selfless ideas no longer command widespread lip-service, let alone respect. We view sacrifice as a sign of weakness. Yet sacrifice remains central to human evolution. No matter where we are or what we are doing, we have the choice of dedicating our efforts to helping others or exalting ourselves.

Back in the 15th century, in a tiny village near Nuremberg, lived a family with 18 children. To keep food on the table, the father, a goldsmith by profession, worked almost 16 hours a day at his trade and any other paying chore he could find. Despite their seemingly hopeless conditions, two of Albrecht Durer Snr children had a dream; they wanted to pursue their talent for art. However, they knew their father could never afford to send either of them to Nuremberg to study at the academy.

After many discussions, the two boys finally worked out a pact. They would toss a coin. The loser would go down into the nearby mines and, with his earnings, support his brother while he attended the academy. Then, when that brother who won the toss completed his studies, he would support the other brother at the academy, either with sales of his artwork or, if necessary, also by labouring in the mines. They tossed a coin on a Sunday morning after church. Albrecht Durer won the toss and went off to

Nuremberg. His brother Albert went down into the dangerous mines and, for the next four years, financed his brother, whose work at the academy was almost an immediate sensation. Albrecht's etchings, his woodcuts, and his oils were far better than those of most of his professors, and by the time he graduated he was beginning to earn considerable fees for his commissioned works.

When the young artist returned to his village, the Durer family held a festive dinner on their lawn to celebrate Albrecht's triumphant homecoming. After a memorable meal, punctuated with music and laughter, Albrecht rose from his honoured position at the head of the table to drink a toast to his beloved brother for the years of sacrifice that had enabled Albrecht to fulfil his ambition. His closing words were: 'And now, Albert, blessed brother of mine, now it is your turn. Now you can go to Nuremberg to pursue your dream and I will take care of you.'

All heads turned in eager expectation to the far end of the table where Albert sat, tears streaming down his face, shaking his lowered head from side to side. 'No ... no ... no,' he sobbed. Finally, Albert rose and wiped the tears from his cheeks. He glanced down the long table at the faces he loved.

Holding his hands close to his right cheek, he said softly, 'No, brother. I cannot go to Nuremberg. It's too late for me. Look what four years in the mines have done to my hands. The bones in every finger have been smashed at least once and lately I've been suffering from arthritis so badly in my right hand that I cannot even hold a glass to return your toast, much less make delicate lines on parchment or canvas with a pen or a brush. No, brother ... for me, it is too late.'

More than 450 years have passed. By now, Albrecht Durer's hundreds of masterful portraits, pen and silver point sketches, water-colours, charcoals, woodcuts and copper engravings hang in every great museum in the world. Of course, most of us are only familiar with one of Albrecht Durer's works. Indeed, many of us will have a reproduction of it hanging in our homes or offices.

To pay homage to Albert for all he had sacrificed, Albrecht Durer painstakingly drew his brother's abused hands with palms together and thin fingers stretched skyward. He called his powerful drawing simply 'Hands', but it has become popularly known as 'The Praying Hands'.

There comes a time when you must stand alone. You must feel confident enough within yourself to follow your own dreams. You must be willing to make sacrifices. You must be capable of changing and rearranging your priorities so that your final goal can be achieved. Sometimes, familiarity and comfort need to be challenged.

There are times when you must take a few extra chances and create your own realities. Be strong enough to at least try to make your life better. Be confident enough that you won't settle for a compromise just to get by. Appreciate yourself by allowing yourself the opportunities to grow, develop, and find your true sense of purpose in this life.

Don't stand in someone else's shadow when it's your sunlight that should lead the way. Work hard at what you like to do and try to overcome all obstacles. Laugh at your mistakes and praise yourself for learning from them. Love your friends and family with your entire being, they are the most important part of your life

A MOMENT IN TIME

The next time you see a copy of that touching creation of the Praying Hands, take a second look. Let it be your reminder, if you still need one, that no one ever makes it alone.

TIME OUT

FIFTY-THREE

MY ENCOUNTER WITH MARA NIVAD–DAVY

I remember one cold morning in India I went to Sealdah Railway station to reserve my ticket for a short holiday to Darjeeling to follow the journey of Mother Teresa's beginnings. It was cold, foggy weather which was unusual for Calcutta. My rickshaw taxi dropped me near the station and I tried to go inside to the ticket counter.

Suddenly, I saw a middle-aged woman, trying to get relief from the cold with a torn blanket, lying on the ground at the entrance of the men's toilet. She was suffering from leprosy as the fingers of her hands were falling off and one of her feet was also hanging by its sinews. She was trying to cover her body with the torn blanket so that no one would see her deformity but she failed every time to do it. She wished for someone to come and help her. So many people crossed by there but no one helped.

I suddenly realised that God sent me to help this person and I quickly ran to help her cover her body. She was barely able to whisper the words, "thank you." I flagged down a taxi and the taxi driver seeing my predicament with the sick woman sped through the streets of Calcutta waving a red flag or handkerchief out the side window of his car so that we could get to the Mother Teresa's house called Kali-ghat which was also known as the house of the dying. I found out in our journey from Sealdah Railway station to the house of the dying that her name was Mara Nivad-Davy.

On that journey she told me her about her life – one of abject poverty and horror.

I carried her from the taxi among the throng of people on the streets of Calcutta into Mother Teresa's house of the dying. I cleared a spot for her on one of the beds. I was standing near her feet and as the Mother Teresa sisters cleaned her and cared for her, I couldn't help notice or stop looking at the fact that half her left foot was missing.

It had been completely eaten away by maggots and as we cleaned it many more maggots were taken out. The bones were sticking out of her foot and some of these had even been worn away because Mara had used her foot to drag her self along because she couldn't walk. The foot was eventually amputated that day and Mara died a few days later surrounded by much love and prayers many of the Mother Teresa sisters present in Kalighat.

That encounter changed me a lot. God gave me the dream to help the poor and those in need in our community and in our world. I realised that a dream is one thing but trying to achieve it is another thing altogether. From that day I promised myself that whatever it took I would help lots of people to live in a caring and loving world. I am still doing my best to try and do that but everyday I need help.

A MOMENT IN TIME

If you see anybody who requires help, don't just pass by. Try to come to their aid. Maybe God sent you to help them. Actually the true story above was an eye opener for me and obviously that incident in my life gave me the opportunity to help a poor woman in need.

FIFTY-FOUR

THE POTATO, THE EGG AND THE COFFEE BEAN

When people experience hard times, it can sometimes seem that it will never end. The dictionary defines adversity as 'a stated, condition or instance of serious or continued difficulty.' People going through adversity are more likely to define it as hell. It is the long drawn-out nature of adversity, rather than brief spells of misfortune, that can crush the human spirit and cause related illnesses such as stress and depression. However, it's also at such times that people can discover their inner resilience and optimism, while having faith that the difficult times will come to an end.

Once upon a time, a daughter complained to her father that her life was miserable and that she didn't know how she was going to make it. She was tired of fighting and struggling all the time. It seemed just as one problem was solved, another one soon followed.

Her father, a chef, took her to the kitchen. He filled three pots with water and placed each on a high fire. Once the three pots began to boil, he placed potatoes in one pot, eggs in the second pot, and ground coffee beans in the third pot. He then let them sit and boil, without saying a word to his daughter. The daughter moaned and impatiently waited, wondering what he was doing. After 20 minutes he turned off the burners. He took the potatoes out of the pot and placed them in a bowl. He pulled the eggs out and placed them in a bowl. He then ladled the coffee out and placed it in a cup.

Turning to her, he asked, "What do you see?"

"Potatoes, eggs, and coffee," she replied.

"Look closer," he said "and touch the potatoes." She did and noted that they were soft. He then asked her to take an egg and break it. After pulling off the shell, she observed the hard-boiled egg. Finally, he asked her to sip the coffee. Its rich aroma brought a smile to her face. "OK, what does this mean?" she asked.

He then explained that the potatoes, the eggs, and coffee beans had faced the same adversity, the boiling water. However, each one reacted differently. The potato went in strong, hard and unrelenting, but in boiling water it became soft and weak. The egg was fragile with the thin outer shell protecting its liquid interior until it was put in the boiling water. Then the inside of the egg became hard. However, the ground coffee beans were unique. After they were exposed to the boiling water, they changed the water and created something new.

"Which are you?" he asked his daughter. "When adversity knocks on your door, how do you respond? Are you a potato, an egg, or a coffee bean?"

A MOMENT IN TIME
In life, things happen around us and things happen to us, but the only thing that truly matters is what happens within us.

FIFTY-FIVE

REMEMBERING THE DUCK

All too often we spend hours and hours dwelling on the negative and fearful things in our lives. Instead, our focus and attention needs to be on the positive, the good, and on thoughts that will move us in the right direction. As the saying goes, "If you pay attention to the darkness, you'll never find the light."

If you study and relive your past experiences, analysing them, and 'getting in touch with your feelings' you will only reinforce those feelings.

If you want to get away from a problem, you should not focus on it. Focus on the good, the positive, the beautiful, the nice. A happy person is fully caught up in the moment and is not thinking about the past or the future.

Too much thinking and analysing just makes a problem worse. Today is a wonderful day; live it in the present. Living in the present is to be aware of what is happening to you, what you are doing and what you are feeling and thinking. It's being conscious of your thoughts and focusing them on the present.

In this way you look at situations as they are, without colouring them with your past experiences. Living in such a way makes it easier to deal with whatever you are doing at the present moment. The old English story or fable that follows about the pet duck will help you understand.

※ ※ ※

There was a little boy visiting his grandparents on their farm. He was given a slingshot to play with out in the woods. He practised in the woods but he could never hit the target. A little discouraged, he headed back for dinner. As he was walking back he saw Nana's pet duck. Just out of impulse, he let the slingshot fly, hit the duck square in the head, and killed it. He was shocked and grieved.

In a panic, he hid the dead duck in the wood pile, only to see his sister watching. Sally had seen it all, but she said nothing. After lunch the next day Nana said, "Sally, let's wash the dishes."

But Sally said: "Nana, Johnny told me he wanted to help in the kitchen." Then she whispered to him, "Remember the duck?"

So Johnny did the dishes. Later that day, Grandad asked if the children wanted to go fishing and Nana said: "I'm sorry but I need Sally to help make supper."

Sally just smiled and said: "Well that's all right because Johnny told me he wanted to help." She whispered again: "Remember the duck?"

So Sally went fishing and Johnny stayed to help. After several days of Johnny doing both his chores and Sally's he couldn't stand it any longer. He came to Nana and confessed that he had killed the duck. Nana knelt down, gave him a hug, and said, "Sweetheart, I know. You see, I was standing at the window and I saw the whole thing. But because I love you, I forgave you. I was just wondering how long you would let Sally make a slave of you."

So whatever is in your past, whatever you have done and the devil keeps throwing it up in your face (lying, debt, fear, hatred, anger, unforgiveness, bitterness etc.) whatever it is, you need to know that God was standing at the window and He saw the whole thing, He has seen your whole life.

He wants you to know that He loves you and that you are forgiven. He's just wondering how long you will let the devil make a slave of you. The great thing about God is that when you ask for forgiveness, He not only forgives you, but He forgets – It is by God's grace and mercy that we are saved.

A MOMENT IN TIME

Go ahead and make a difference in someone's life today and always remember: "God is at the window." Also remember that today is a gift and that's why it is called the present.

TIME OUT

FIFTY-SIX

PEEK-A-BOO

We were the only family with children in the restaurant. I sat Sophie in a high chair. Suddenly, Sophie squealed with glee and said, "Hi there." She pounded her baby hands on the high chair tray. Her eyes were full of laughter as she giggled with merriment. I looked around and saw the source of her merriment. It was a man who wore dirty and ripped clothes with his toes poking out of would-be shoes. His shirt was dirty and his hair was unwashed. He smelled. "Hi kiddo," the man said to Sophie. My wife and I exchanged looks, "What do we do?" Sophie continued to laugh and answer, "Hi there."

Everyone in the restaurant looked at us. The old man was creating a nuisance with my beautiful baby. Our meal came and the man began shouting: "Do you know peek-a-boo? Hey, look, she knows peek-a-boo." Nobody thought the old man was cute. He was obviously drunk. My wife and I were a bit embarrassed. We ate in silence, all except for Sophie, who was running through her repertoire for the admiring old man, who in turn, reciprocated with his cute comments. We finally got through the meal and headed for the door. My wife went to pay the bill and told me to meet her at the car.

The old man sat between me and the door. "Lord, just let me out of here before he speaks to me or Sophie," I prayed. As I drew closer to the man, I turned my back trying to sidestep him. As I did, Sophie leaned over my arm, reaching with both arms to the old man. Before I could stop her, Sophie had propelled herself from my arms to the man's.

Suddenly a very old smelly man and a very young baby showed their care for one another. Sophie in an act of total trust and love laid her tiny head upon the man's ragged shoulder. The man's eyes filled with tears. His aged hands full of grime and pain cradled my baby and stroked her back. No two beings have ever loved so deeply for so short a time.

I stood awestruck.

The old man rocked and cradled Sophie in his arms and his eyes opened and set squarely on mine. He said in a commanding voice, "You take care of this baby."

Somehow I managed to say, "I will." He prised Sophie from his chest unwillingly as though he were in pain. I received my baby, and the man said: "God bless you, you've given me a special gift."

I muttered 'thanks'. With Sophie in my arms, I ran for the car. My wife was wondering why I was crying and holding Sophie so tightly and why I was saying: "My God, please forgive me." I had just witnessed real genuine love shown through the innocence of a tiny child who made no judgment; a child who saw a soul, and me a father who saw a dirty ragged old man.

I was an adult who was blind, holding a child who was not. The ragged old man unwittingly had reminded me that some of the greatest lessons in life are taught to us by children.

A MOMENT IN TIME

Never underestimate the power of your actions. With one small gesture you can change a person's life and remember to always treat others the way you would like to be treated yourself.

FIFTY-SEVEN

THE WHITE ROSE OF CHRISTMAS

The following is a story I came across recently called the White Rose of Christmas. It's a story of a husband and father whose wife and daughter died tragically. It's about Christmas and the real love children have for their parents and loved ones.

'I hurried into the local shop to grab some last minute Christmas gifts. Out of the corner of my eye, I saw a little boy holding a doll. I wondered who the doll was for. "Are you sure I don't have enough money?" he asked his aunt. "You know you don't have enough money," she said, before asking him to wait as she hurried to get some other items. Now curious, I asked the boy who the doll was for. "It is the doll my sister wanted so badly for Christmas. She just knew that Santa would bring it," he said.

I told him that maybe Santa was going to bring it. "No, Santa can't go where my sister is. I have to give the doll to my Mammy to take to her," he said. I asked him where his sister was.

He looked at me with the saddest eyes and said, "She has gone to be with Jesus. My Daddy says that Mammy is going to have to go with her. I told my Daddy to tell Mammy not to go yet. I told him to tell her to wait until I got back from the store." Then he showed me some photos he'd taken of himself. "I want my Mammy to take this with her so she doesn't ever forget me. I wish Mammy did not have to leave me, but Daddy says she needs to be with my sister," he said. The little boy lowered his head and grew very quiet. While he was not looking, I reached into my wallet and pulled out a handful of notes. I asked the little boy, "Shall we count that money one more time?"

I slipped my money in with his and we began to count it. Of

course, it was plenty for the doll. He softly said, "Thank you I have enough money. I just prayed that I would to get enough money to buy this doll and now I have enough to buy the doll and a rose for my Mammy. She loves white roses."

A few minutes later his aunt came back and I walked away. I could not keep from thinking about the little boy as I finished my shopping in a totally different spirit than when I had started.

I remembered a story I had seen in the newspaper about a drunk driver hitting a car and killing a little girl. It said the mother was in a serious condition and the family was deciding on whether to remove the life support.

Two days later, I read that the family had disconnected the life support and the young woman had died. I could not forget the little boy and just kept wondering if the two were somehow connected. Later that day, I bought some white roses and took them to the funeral home. There was the young mum in her coffin holding a lovely white rose, the beautiful doll and the picture of the little boy in the store. I left there in tears, my life changed forever.'

> **A MOMENT IN TIME**
> *Make sure you get your fill of the true spirit of Christmas and not the spirit that can cause much sadness.*

FIFTY-EIGHT

ATTITUDE IS KING

I believe we should all take a few moments everyday to reflect upon our blessings in life. Far too often we get caught up in the unimportant rather than what is really important which are the many blessings and wonderful family and friends that surround us.

If you were to live in the developing world countries, you would see what blessings you already possess. Over 70 per cent of the world's population lives without electricity, running water, healthcare, and in many cases not enough food to eat. If you had been born in these areas, your home would be in a slum area with no running water, no electricity, no television, no i-phones, no computers but much of this wouldn't make any difference anyway because you would be illiterate.

Your children's education would no longer be important because they would have to work simply to help you put enough food on the table to keep everyone alive. The nearest healthcare, if there was any, might be 50 miles or more away and likely you would have to walk to get to it. Probably one of the most amazing things is that your life expectancy, instead of being 75, would now be cut to a mere 50 years old. Hopefully, you would not be a resident of the countries that suffers from wars and droughts, in which case, your life expectancy would be much shorter.

So every morning stop for a few minutes and reflect upon the many blessings that you have. Think about the wonderful family and friends that surround you. Think about the freedoms that you enjoy and reflect upon the fact that no matter how bad your troubles may seem that you are far better off than two-thirds of the people on this planet. As the saying goes: "Your Attitude is everything!"

"There once was a woman who woke up one morning, looked in the mirror, and noticed she had only three hairs on her head. 'Well', she said, 'I think I'll braid my hair today?' So she did and she had a wonderful day. The next day she woke up, looked in the mirror and saw that she had only two hairs on her head. 'I think I'll part my hair down the middle today?' she said. So she did and she had a grand day. The next day she woke up, looked in the mirror and noticed that she had only one hair on her head. 'Well,' she said, 'today I'm going to wear my hair in a pony tail.' So she did and she had a fun day. The next day she woke up, looked in the mirror and noticed that there wasn't a single hair on her head. 'YEA!' she exclaimed, 'I don't have to fix my hair today.' Attitude is everything."

A MOMENT IN TIME
Adopt an attitude of gratitude for the blessings in your life and you will find yourself much happier with the things you have now.

FIFTY-NINE

TODAY IS THE FIRST DAY OF THE REST OF YOUR LIFE

There is a song that goes 'Beginning today my mornings are yours full of hope and joy...', well this week as you wake from your sleep remind yourself that today is the preparation for the rest of your life. Life is and can be full of hardships, sorrows, and trials. The only way to beat these odds is to face up to them as the challenges of life and continue improving yourself.

Don't waste your time with idleness, cowardliness and worry. Instead, use it as an opportunity for improving your life. Take positive charge of your mind and be careful and tactful in your words when you are talking with other people.

Recently we've heard of people who have died by suicide and that life and death can be in the power of others' words. Take good care of your health for it is your only investment in reaching your goals and dreams in life.

Where possible, put others first and serve them honestly with love and care for these are your only chances to share the love, kindness and blessings from above. Teach yourself to be compassionate, humble, loving, and open in dealing with people. I've learned from my parents, grandparents, teachers, close friends and from the elderly who have paved the way for us that being a compassionate, humble, loving, and open person is the best cure in the healing of wounds.

Teach yourself the importance of hard work, honesty, sincerity, time management, initiative, planning, creativeness, determination, patience, persistence, enthusiasm, cooperation, faith, and trust, for these are the secrets of success in any field of work.

Embrace all the hardships, sorrows, and trials as challenges and stepping-stones for success. It will nurture your character for your character is the only shield to protect and cover your reputation.

Improve yourself in whatever way you can as it will teach you the importance of self-respect and self-discipline; these are the foundations of success. Practise being your original self. Today is your only chance to prove and show the world that you are unique, created to bring productivity into this world that we live in. Remove from your dictionary such empty words as defeat, failure, impossible, hopeless, and retreat.

Finally, beginning today, make your loving God whoever you conceive that to be, a partner in your every plan and decisions in your life. With God you can do all things that others think and see as impossible.

A MOMENT IN TIME

Open your heart and mind to all that is good and you'll find yourself being one of the happiest and most successful persons.

SIXTY

EXPERIENCING NATURE SPEAKING TO YOUR SOUL

Recently I was out hiking in one of my favourite places in Ireland, Roundstone in Connemara on the beaches and hills around 'Dogs Bay' with my brother-in-law, Gavin. We stopped to view the ocean stretching on forever beneath and out in front of us. We noticed a family of four dolphins very close by. We sat down by the hill edge and enjoyed viewing the dolphin family swimming very close by us as we took some fantastic photographs.

It is only when we slow down a bit that we really see and experience nature around us. Stopping and being still in nature is a way we can connect to it, precisely because we see, hear and experience it more. Taking time to be still, quieter and look around connects us to our natural surroundings. Seeing that special sunset, beautiful view or dolphins leaping like I did in 'Dogs Bay' makes spending time in nature even more fulfilling. It makes us more connected and more grounded and takes us to a different slower pace of life.

Hiking that day in 'Dogs Bay' was beautiful, peaceful, energising and relaxing as we felt the peace and quiet. Spending time in and with nature is healing and brings calmness into our lives. We can walk or run in nature, sit in nature and swim in the waters of nature. We can do this out in the wilderness or in our local park. There is something awe-inspiring about nature and we can feel most connected to this feeling in those wilderness places; the forests, rivers, waterfalls, oceans and mountains and we have them in abundance here in our beautiful country of Ireland.

Yet this awe and inspiration is there in every space where

nature is, from your garden to your local park, the prom walk by the sea at Salthill or the trail through the small wooded areas, forests and mountains all around Galway.

Nature is part of us and yet we can spend so little time in it. When we do we feel a reconnection which is more than just the fresh air, exercise or beautiful sights, it also speaks to something in our heart and soul and helps give our life some real spirit.

A MOMENT IN TIME
Strive to spend more time being aware of nature and let it speak to your heart and soul so that it can give your life some real and nourishing spirit.

SIXTY-ONE

IT'S OK TO CRY

At times during my life I've been overwhelmed with sadness and even though I am a positive person, no thought seems to be able to get me out of that 'dark place' at that moment When I am in this 'dark place', I can't even think straight and even though there are plenty of things that I love to do, at that moment nothing seem to be interesting.

And it's at moments like these that I have learnt that 'it's ok to cry.' To feel this sadness is ok. Sometimes we think crying is a sign of weakness. Crying is a sign that we have a heart. That we care. Also there is a healing power in crying. The power of being able to release that feeling.

When you release it and take the time to come to terms with it, you're able to move on. But if you keep it bottled up, it comes out in negative feelings. So let yourself cry if you are sad. Let your heart express that feeling. You will be happier when you do, because you are releasing it. It will make room to have other feelings that are happy to come into your heart, mind and soul. The following old spiritual story can shine some light on what I am trying to say.

Once, there was an island where all the feelings lived: Happiness, Sadness, and all of the others, including Love. One day it was announced to the feelings that the island would sink, so all repaired their boats and left. Love was the only one who stayed. Love wanted to persevere until the last moment. When the island was almost sinking, Love decided to ask for help.

Richness was passing by Love in a grand boat. Love said: "Richness, can you take me with you?"

Richness answered: "No I can't. There is a lot of gold and silver in my boat. There is no room."

Love decided to ask Vanity, who was also passing by in a beautiful vessel: "Vanity, please help me."

"I can't help you, Love. You are all wet and might damage my boat," Vanity answered.

Sadness was close by so Love asked for help: "Sadness let me go with you."

"Oh Love, I am so sad that I need to be by myself."

Happiness passed by Love too, but she was so happy that she did not even hear when Love called her.

Suddenly, there was a voice: "Come, Love, I will take you." It was an elder. Love felt so overjoyed that he forgot to ask the elder her name. When they arrived at dry land, the elder went her own way. Love, realising how much he owed the elder, asked Knowledge, another elder: 'Who helped me?"

"It was Time,' Knowledge answered. "Time?" asked Love. "But why did Time help me?"

Knowledge smiled with deep wisdom and answered: "Because only Time is capable of understanding how great Love is."

A MOMENT IN TIME

Don't be afraid to cry for help. It will give you more room in your heart to feel better things. It's just like forgiveness. It frees our own hearts more than the person that we forgive.

SIXTY-TWO

FOLLOW YOUR HEART

I have a friend named Noel who owns a farm in the midlands. At times he has let me use his farm to put on events to raise money for children's projects in Africa.

The last time I was there he introduced me by saying: "I want to tell you why I let Ronan use my farm. It all goes back to a story about a young man who was the son of a poor horse trainer who would go from stable to stable, racetrack to racetrack and farm to farm, training horses. As a result, the boy's school career was continually interrupted. When he was close to his Leaving Cert year, he was asked to write a paper about what he wanted to be and do when he grew up.

"That night he wrote a seven-page paper describing his ambition of owning a horse farm some day. He wrote in great detail and he even drew a diagram of a 200-acre farm, showing the location of all the buildings, the stables and the track. Then he drew a detailed floor plan for a 4,000-square-foot house that would sit on a 200-acre dream farm.

"He put his heart into the project and the next day he handed it in to his teacher. Two days later he received his paper back. On the front page was a large red 'F' with a note that read: 'See me after class.'

"The boy with the dream went to see the teacher after class and asked, 'Why did I receive an F?'

The teacher said: 'This is an unrealistic dream for a young boy like you. You have no money. You come from a poor family. You have no resources. Owning a horse farm requires a lot of money. You have to buy the land. You have to pay for the original breeding stock and later you'll have to pay large stud fees.

There's no way you could ever do it.' Then the teacher added: 'If you will rewrite this paper with a more realistic goal, I will reconsider your grade.'

"The boy went home and thought about it long and hard. He asked his father what he should do. His father said: 'Look, son, you have to make up your own mind on this. However, I think it is a very important decision for you.' Finally, after sitting with it for a week, the boy turned in the same paper, making no changes at all. He stated: 'You can keep the F and I'll keep my dream.'"

Noel then turned to the assembled group and said: "I tell you this story because you are sitting in my 4,000-square-foot house in the middle of my 200-acre horse farm. I still have that school paper framed over the fireplace."

He added: "The best part of the story is that two summers ago that same schoolteacher brought 30 young students to camp out on my farm for a week."

When the teacher was leaving, he said: "Look, Noel, I can tell you this now. When I was your teacher, I was something of a dream stealer. Fortunately you had enough gumption not to give up on yours.

"Don't let anyone steal your dreams. Follow your heart, no matter what."

A MOMENT IN TIME

Never doubt yourself or your dreams or the genuine goodness of another human being, as soon as you feel even vaguely inspired, get up and take some action.

SIXTY-THREE

HAUNTING IMAGES

Most mornings while I lived in Ethiopia, I had my breakfast in a small street vendor's tent in a place called Kotebe. I'd watch the world go by and the deluge of people was never ending going up and down the street. On one of those mornings, I noticed a little girl begging for some food. The street vendor opened up his container and showed the girl that it was all but gone. The girl then begged for some Injera, which is the local food of Ethiopia.

The vendor was willing enough to give the last scraps of food but the girl had no plate. However looking around for a while, she reached into the refuse bin where she found some paper. She collected the rather watery Injera in the paper, with some spillage on her dirty rags that once used to be a dress and left. I realised then to my horror that the girl was not alone – she had her family, possibly siblings and this watery Injera with nothing in it but some heavily diluted gravy was to be the family breakfast that morning.

Some of the images from my years working in the developing world have faded from my memory but I think that this one will never fade away. I saw the despair and lack of hope on the little girl's face when she peered into the almost empty container and how her face glowed with delight at the sight of the watery Injera which offered little in terms of nutrients.

I often recall the quote of Mahatma Gandhi which says: "I will give you a talisman. Whenever you are in doubt, or when the self becomes too much with you, apply the following test. Recall the face of the poorest and the weakest person you have seen and ask yourself if the step you contemplate is going to be of any use to them. Will they gain anything by it? Will it restore them to a control over their own life and destiny? In other words, will it lead to freedom for the hungry and spiritually starving millions? Then you will find your doubts melt away".

We should do all we can to stand up for the future of our greatest treasure – our children – on whose shoulders we have already put our future existence. By being positive where we can, by been supportive of ourselves and our communities, by helping and by showing leadership, we can give true hope to our children. Let's do it.

A MOMENT IN TIME

If we believe in the goodness of one another then we will do whatever we can to care and love everyone in our communities as much as we humanly can.

SIXTY-FOUR

TAKE CUSTODY OF YOUR TONGUE

Gossip is something many of us do on a daily basis. Gossip seems harmless on the surface but it can be the source of negative things in people's lives. Gossip is certainly not giving love, it's the exact opposite.

This is a great thought I heard from a priest saying mass in a mission in Angola called 'Who Am I'. "I am more deadly than the screaming shell of the cannon. I win without killing. I tear down homes, break hearts, and wreck lives. I travel on the wings of the wind. No innocence is strong enough to intimidate me, no purity pure enough to daunt me. I have no regard for truth, no respect for justice, no mercy for the defenceless. My victims are as numerous as the sands of the sea and often as innocent. I never forget and seldom forgive. My name is Gossip."

If a person who gossips could feel for themselves the pain, the anger, the humiliation and hopelessness that resulted, I'm certain gossip would subside.

In the Benedictine monastic tradition, there is a spiritual practice called keeping custody of your tongue. The idea is to consciously pay attention to what you say at all times. It's okay to speak your mind and even to express anger but you must do so with awareness that harsh words can be very harmful. Keeping custody of your tongue is not an easy practice. Be patient with yourself. The only way to break a habit of careless and harmful words is to work on it day by day with honest intention.

Just consider the consequences of not paying attention to what you say.

❈ ❈ ❈

In a small community, one fellow is known as the town gossip. He has thoughtlessly told and retold some stories that have caused others to feel pain and shame. When his local curate confronts him about the damage he has done, the man is sorry for being so hurtful. He asks what he can do to make amends. The curate tells him to take some pillows out into a field, to cut them open and to shake all the feathers out into the field. The man thanks the curate and runs off to do what he said.

Later, he returns and reports that the wind has taken the feathers to all parts of the field. The curate tells him this is good and now he must go back to the field and collect all the feathers. The gossip knows that is an impossible task. Hurtful words once spoken cannot be retrieved. It's better to take custody of your tongue in the first place.

A MOMENT IN TIME
Remember that sometimes the strongest people are the ones who love beyond all faults, cry behind closed doors and fight battles that nobody knows about and yet they are gossiped about. Take custody of your tongue in your dealings with others.

SIXTY-FIVE

THE GIFT OF KINDNESS

Abraham Lincoln once said: "Kindness is the only service that will stand the storm of life and not wash out. It will wear well and be remembered long after the prism of politeness or the complexion of courtesy has faded away. When I am gone, I hope it can be said of me that I plucked a thistle and planted a flower wherever I thought a flower would grow."

In the quest to create a gentler, more loving world, kindness is the easiest tool we can use. Though it is easy to overlook opportunities to be kind, our lives are full of situations in which we can be helpful, considerate, thoughtful and friendly to loved ones as well as strangers. The touching, selfless acts of kindness that have the most profoundly uplifting effects are often the simplest: A word of praise, a gentle touch, a helping hand, a gesture of courtesy or a smile.

Such small kindnesses represent an unconditional form of love that we are free to give or withhold at will. When you give the gift of kindness, whether in the form of assistance, concern, or friendliness, your actions create a beacon of happiness and hope that warms people's hearts. The components of kindness are compassion, respect and generosity. Put simply, kindness is the conscious act of engaging others in a positive way without asking whether those individuals deserve to be treated kindly.

All living beings thrive on kindness. A single, sincere compliment can turn a person's entire world around. Holding a door, or thanking someone who has held a door for you, can inspire others to practise politeness and make already kind individuals feel good about their efforts. Smiling at people you meet, even those who make you feel like frowning, can turn a dreary encounter into a delightful one, for both of you. Every kind act has a positive influence on the individual who has performed the act as well as on the recipient, regardless of whether the act is acknowledged.

Kindness brings about more kindness and slowly but surely makes a positive impact on humanity. You'll discover that each act of kindness you engage in makes the world, in some small way, a better place.

As the saying goes, "Many people will walk in and out of your life, but only true friends will leave footprints in your heart. To handle yourself, use your head; to handle others, use your heart. Anger is only one letter short of danger. If someone betrays once, it is his fault; if he betrays you twice, it is your fault. Great minds discuss ideas; average minds discuss events; small minds discuss people. He who loses money, loses much; he who loses a friend, loses much more; he who loses faith, loses all. Learn from the mistakes of others; you can't live long enough to make them all yourself. Friends, you and me ... You brought another friend ... and we started our group ... our circle of friends ... and like a circle ... there is no beginning or end. Yesterday is history. Tomorrow is mystery. Today is a gift."

A MOMENT IN TIME

Practise genuine kindness as much as you can in your daily life and 'plant flowers' wherever you can.

SIXTY-SIX

THE REAL SPIRIT OF CHRISTMAS

The following story I heard from a friend about a family who decided a long time ago that rather than buying presents for one another at Christmas they would buy something more meaningful that would fit into the spirit of a Christ-filled Christmas.

"It's just a white envelope stuck among the branches of our Christmas tree. No name or no inscription. It has peeked through the branches of our tree for many years now. It all began because my wife Siobhan hated Christmas. Not the true meaning of Christmas, but the commercial aspects of it.

Knowing she felt this way, one year I decided to bypass the presents. I reached for something special just for Siobhan. The inspiration came in an unusual way. Our son Kevin, who was 12 that year, was boxing at at the school he attended. Shortly before Christmas, there was a non-league match against a team sponsored by a church, mostly asylum seekers.

These youngsters, dressed in runners so ragged that shoestrings seemed to be the only thing holding them together, presented a sharp contrast to our boys in their fancy sportswear and new boxing shoes. As the match began, I was alarmed to see that the other team was boxing without proper headgear that protected a boxer's head. It was a luxury they could not afford. We beat them in every weight class.

Siobhan shook her head sadly. "I wish just one of them could have won," she said. "They have a lot of potential, but losing like this could take the heart right out of them." That's when the idea for her present came. That afternoon, I went to a local sports shop and bought an assortment of boxing headgear and shoes and sent them anonymously to the church team. On Christmas Eve, I placed the envelope on the tree, the note inside telling Siobhan what I had done and that this was her gift from me. Her smile was the brightest thing about Christmas that year.

Every Christmas that followed, I kept the tradition, one year sending a group of seriously unwell youngsters to a football game, another year a cheque to a pair of elderly brothers whose home had just burned to the ground, and so on. The envelope became the highlight of our Christmas. It was always the last thing opened on Christmas morning and our children would stand in anticipation as their mother opened the envelope to reveal its contents. Over the years the envelope never lost its allure.

We lost Siobhan last year. When Christmas rolled around, I was still so wrapped in grief that I barely got the tree up. But Christmas Eve found me placing an envelope on the tree, and in the morning, it was joined by three more. Each of our children, unbeknownst to the others, had placed an envelope on the tree for their mother. The tradition has grown and someday will expand even further with our grandchildren standing around the tree with wide-eyed anticipation watching as their parents take down the envelope. Siobhan's spirit, like the Christmas spirit, will always be with us."

A MOMENT IN TIME

Remember to "give" in a Christ-like manner. After all, he is the reason for the season and the true "Christmas spirit".

SIXTY-SEVEN

VALUING OUR ELDERLY

In African and Asian tribal cultures the elderly play an important role. They are the keepers of their tribe's memories and the holders of wisdom. As such, the elderly are honoured and respected members of tribes because they have paved the way for the future for their young.

In our modern cultures, however, this is often not the case. Many elderly people say they feel ignored, left out and disrespected. This is a sad commentary on modernization and urbanization but it doesn't have to be this way. We can change this situation by taking the time to examine our attitudes about the elderly.

Modern societies tend to be obsessed with the ideas of newness, youth and progress. Scientific studies tell us how to do everything – from the way we raise our kids to what we need to eat for breakfast. As a result, the wisdom that is passed down from older generations is often disregarded.

Grandparents and retired persons have more than enough information to offer the world. Their maturity and experience allows for a larger perspective on life and we can learn a lot from talking to them. It's a shame that society doesn't do more to allow our older population to continue to feel productive for the rest of their lives.

We can all play a part in changing this. Perhaps you could help facilitate a mentorship programme that would allow children to be tutored by the elderly or retirement groups. The elderly are invariably wonderful storytellers and creating programmes where they could share their real life experiences with others is another way to educate and inspire other generations.

Maybe you don't really listen to the elderly because you hold the belief that their time has passed and they are too old to understand what you are going through. You may even realise that you don't have any relationships with older people. Try to understand why and how our cultural perception of the elderly influences the way you perceive them.

To end this topic I want to share with you an old Irish Celtic prayer about Wisdom.

'People can be unreasonable, illogical, and self-centred, Forgive them anyway. If you are kind, people may accuse you of ulterior motives; be kind anyway.

If you are successful, you will win some false friends and some true enemies; succeed anyway. If you are honest and frank, people may cheat you; be honest and frank anyway.

What you spend years building, someone could destroy overnight; build anyway. If you find serenity and happiness, they may be jealous; be happy anyway.

The good you do today, people will often forget tomorrow; do good anyway. Give the world the best you have, and it may never be enough; give the world the best you've got anyway.

You see, in the final analysis, it is between you and God; It never was between you and them anyway.'

A MOMENT IN TIME

Look around you and reach out to someone who is elderly, even if you are just saying hello and making small talk. Resolve to be more aware of the elderly: They are the pioneers that came before us and paved the way for our future.

SIXTY-EIGHT

REDISCOVERING YOUR LOVE

The first thing I did each day during my time working on the streets of Calcutta in India was to attend mass in Mother Teresa convent, before heading out onto the streets where I worked with street children, lepers and the dying. At one of these masses an Indian priest gave a beautiful sermon. If I can remember properly it was about the following family and their joy of resurrecting their love.

One day a child got the toy he had hoped for. He hugged it as if it was priceless and agreed when told that, as it was very expensive, his parents would not be able to afford another one. He called his friends and showed them his new toy. But the elation did not last long. After a few weeks, one of his friends got the latest toy available the one that was now the most sought after. The child lost interest in his toy, and though his mother tried to explain that his toy was a very good one, he looked away and cried. The toy, now rejected, remained forgotten in a corner.

The child's mother had her own problems. After much planning and saving, she had just gotten her new home and worked hard to ensure it would be the pride of the community. This was until a new house was built close by. This new house was undoubtedly the most modern. The owner invited her around and showed her inside. When she went back to her own house, she looked at it anew and her heart sank. The house looked common and was not worth any attention or special care. From that moment on, she lost interest in her own home and it became dirty. Her husband noticed the change and gently inquired. His wife told him she was no longer interested in the house because the neighbours house was better. He tried to explain to her that their house was a very good one. But the woman remained silent and cried.

The woman's husband had personal problems too. His wife was beautiful and he was madly in love with her but his friends had young wives and some of them were very beautiful. As he came to know them, his interest in his wife diminished and his feelings changed. A growing coldness crept between them. His wife tried to talk to him, but he remained silent.

One day the child's eye fell on the old abandoned toy. He started playing with it contentedly. He had not noticed that the door of his room was slightly ajar and his mother was looking at him with loving curiosity. She felt happy in her heart that her child had made friends again with his old toy, and she smiled to herself in silence. The next day, as she was sitting alone in her home, she noticed how dusty and dirty it was. She rose to her feet began tidying the house. She had rediscovered her interest in her house and once more she became the efficient wife she used to be. As her husband approached the house, he noticed his wife going enthusiastically about her chores and at once rejoiced. He felt happy that his wife had reconciled herself with the house and he smiled to himself in silence. The next day, when the husband and wife were seated in their sitting room, the husband looked at his wife and suddenly realised again what a beautiful woman she was. In that moment, he realised he loved her more than ever. He went to her and took her in his arms.

THOUGHT OF THE WEEK

As your thought for this week, rediscover the good in your life. Resurrect it, cherish it and hold on to it because life is short.

SIXTY-NINE

MY WORST DAY IS HER BEST DAY EVER

When it comes to blessings, make no mistake about it, we are incredibly blessed, you and I. However that doesn't mean that life isn't tough sometimes for all of us. We often get caught up in the reality of our world and forget our blessings. Illness, financial woes, martial and family strife are enough to temporarily blind anyone to the blessings they enjoy. For some, it's hard to rejoice and be glad simply because their team is down by two goals in the second half of the match.

On the other hand, it takes a really bad day for others to lose touch with their gladness. Still, life has a way of dealing us all with a few bad days in our life now and then.

There is an old adage that goes, 'When you're up to your tail end in alligators, it's hard to remember the objective was to drain the swamp.'

There is a way for pretty much anyone to find comfort in his or her blessings at even the lowest and most difficult times. Ever since I gained this understanding, whenever I am at one of my low points, I apply this method and right away I am once again able to feel blessed and to rejoice and be glad in those blessings.

The method is about perspective and not entirely unlike the old saying: 'I felt bad because I had no shoes until I met a man who had no feet.'

When we are stuck in the misery of our moment, we become so consumed by it and the troubles take on such proportion, that we become unable to see the entirety of our world. By creating contrast, things can take on a whole new look.

❀ ❀ ❀

This is what I do. I think about Berela. She is 25 years old and lives in small village outside the town of Awaza, in Ethiopia. Not so long ago, she watched in horror as her husband and her brother were brutally beaten and killed along with others from her village.

Following the murders, she was savagely beaten then raped repeatedly by a band of thugs. There was no food and no water. In Berela's arms is her young daughter. They are both starving to death. By tomorrow her daughter could be dead and there is absolutely nothing Berela can do to prevent it.

As I focus on Berela and absorb her reality, one thing becomes incredibly clear. This may be the absolute worse day of my life but it's also so remarkably wonderful that it's beyond Berela's ability to imagine as one of her best days ever.

Think about that for a moment. For Berela and for millions of people throughout the world, in places like Darfur and Burma, my 'worst day ever' is so good, it's beyond their ability to dare to hope for as their 'best day ever. Whatever day Berela imagines as her 'best day ever' is pretty bleak by comparison.

No matter how awful you think things are in your life at this moment, the fact you are reading this tells me there are a lot of people in this world who can't imagine having it as good as you do right now. A few moments with Berela is all it takes to get my mind right and to help me to know I am blessed.'

A MOMENT IN TIME

Be thankful for your blessings and realise your trials can also be a blessing. Then reach out and share your gladness with someone who is struggling to help them find their gladness.

SEVENTY

MAKE THE MOST OF EVERY OCCASION

Recently while attending a friend's wedding in Connemara, I found myself thinking about the standard thoughts people associate with the word 'celebration'.

These included parties, people, fun, laughter, championship and election wins, gala balls/dances, song, music, drink, food and, usually, more food. Perhaps, even applause and awards. Dressing up or even dressing down. Sleeping too little, maybe even not sleeping at all. Images of people engaged in conversations with other people or even bearing witness to something very special and unique, such as one of our own being made leader of our country.

Weddings are celebrations too. A couple standing side by side at the front of a small church, filled with the excitement and trepidation of a life about to be journeyed together, with friends and family bearing witness.

A child's first birthday is a celebration I recently enjoyed. One large candle on a cake, one glowing smiling face and two small hands, along with lots of other small hands from new friends, reaching out at new things.

Other celebrations are less noticeable.

The smile from the shop attendant who gives you your daily paper. The concerned and thoughtful questions of your family doctor, your local garda or local curate. The patience of the person behind us in the queue as we sort out our financial queries with the bank assistant. The chef in the local restaurant who remembers how you like your food or knows that you want a baby dinner and want it ready as quick as possible. Or, as I found recently, the stranger in the doctor's waiting room that entertains your energetic and restless youngster while you wait your turn.

These frequently occurring moments – if we pay attention to them and honour them – fill our hearts and touch our souls. They are moments that invite us to feel what it is to be human in our ordinary everyday lives, in the presence of another equally ordinary human being, in the creation of a magical moment, whatever you are wearing and whoever you are with.

A MOMENT IN TIME

Think of something important that has happened in your life, and celebrate it this week with family and friends. Life is so short, it is important to make the most of every occasion.

~ ACKNOWLEDGEMENTS ~

I was delighted when my close friend Andrew Downes agreed to do the cover photographs to complement the written thoughts in this book. I was also equally delighted when Hilary Martyn of *The Galway Independent* and well-known journalist and publisher PJ Cunningham came on board to edit the thoughts and Joe Coyle agreed to layout the book for me.

I would also like to thank my friend Des Kenny of Kenny's Bookshop for his foreword and my dear friend Fr. Niall Ahern for his introduction. It's a privilege to have both of them contributing to Time Out.

I would like to dedicate this book to my beautiful wife Jacqui, daughters Mia and Sophie, my mother and father Mary and Ricey, my brother Darragh, my sisters Lavinia and Oonagh and to all my family, friends and colleagues over the years who have supported me in some way throughout my life.

To Andrew, Anna, Roan, Alice and Lily Downes for their support and friendship. I would also like to dedicate this book to the memory of my close and dear friend Donal Rabbette who I will hold forever in my thoughts.

I would also like to dedicate this book to the memory of my wonderful father-in-law Gerard O'Grady, to the memory of my beautiful aunt Catherine Phelan and to the special memory of my Nana and Grandad Scully and Granny and Grandad Phelan for all that they did for us as family and the great love and inspiration they gave to us with their example of a life lived out in total love for us all.

To my dear friend David Lohan of Lohans, Prospect Hill, Galway who made the publishing of this book possible, I will always be grateful to you David for giving us this opportunity. You are a true light to so many in a world that is dark at times. Thank you so much David from the bottom of my heart and may your own spirit and goodness continue to soar.

To PJ and Rosemary Cunningham of Ballpoint Press for believing in me and for supporting me not just on this project but by being second parents to me and helping to shape me into the person I am today.

I would also like to thank Paul Galvin, Ralph O'Gorman, Ricey Scully, Frank Downes and family, Anna Downes and family, Dick Donovan, the O'Grady family, Kevin Duffy, Paul Tannian, Mark Shaughnessy, Liam Curran, Orla Curran, Alan Kerins, Ray Jordan, Ciara Tallon, Willie Galvin, Micheal O Fioghil, Michael Grealy, George Jacob, Ger Scully, Sean O Gradaigh and Declan Dooley for their valued opinions.

And to Fr. Colm Hogan, Fr. Eamon Kelly, Fr. Frank Duhig, Adrian McGrath, Fearghal Murphy, Ritchie Donovan, Niall McNeilis, Donal Lyons, Sean O Leidghin, Brian and Mary Cowen, Barry Cowen, Danny and Nuala Rabbette, Paul Rabbette, Brian and Lorraine Monroe, Lorraine O'Hanlon, Dervil Dolan, The Meyrick Hotel, Chris and Eavann Farrell, Gary Monroe, Sean Campbell, Gavin Colclough, Damien Doyle, Corah Caples and all my colleagues in Self Help Africa for all your help, advice and support.

Finally, I would like to thank all our family, friends and colleagues who were and are a great source of inspiration to me in everything I try to achieve in life.

I hope and pray that I will someday be able to repay them for all their love and support. Until then you can rest assured you will always be in my prayers and thoughts.

CHOSEN CHARITIES FOR THE PROCEEDS OF THIS BOOK

SELF HELP AFRICA

Self Help Africa is an Irish development agency that has been working for the past 30 years to eradicate hunger and poverty, and support African farmers to earn more from their land.

Established in the aftermath of the catastrophic Ethiopian Famine of 1984, Self Help Africa focuses its efforts primarily on small-scale farming communities. That's because up to 80 per cent of people in Africa rely on the land to make a living.

The organisation works only with local staff and partners in eight African countries, and over the past few decades has helped millions of rural Africans to grow more, to earn more, and to develop new enterprise and ways of making a living to support their families.

Self Help Africa focuses particular attention on rural women – because African women do up to 70% of the work on small farms, yet they currently receive as little as 5% of the available support, and own just 2% of the farm land – which just isn't fair.

To find out more visit: www.selfhelpafrica.org

IRISH GUIDE DOGS FOR THE BLIND

Irish Guide Dogs for the Blind is Ireland's national charity dedicated to helping persons who are blind or vision impaired and families of children with autism to achieve improved mobility and independence. Our vision is a future where persons who are blind, vision impaired and disabled achieve independence and dignity through our world-class dog and ancillary services. Our Mission is to provide the highest quality of services in partnership with our clients while planning for the future and valuing clients, volunteers and each other.

We receive more than 80 per cent of our income through voluntary donations and fundraising through a network of volunteers across the country. It will cost more than €4 million to run our organisation this year. Our National Headquarters and Training Centre is located on the Model Farm Road, two miles outside Cork City. All our training programmes are run at this location. Some of our courses last up to three weeks with clients staying at the centre for the duration of their training. Full aftercare is provided for all clients in their home and community.

See www.guidedogs.ie for further information.